# Instant

# INSPIRATION

# Instant INSPIRATION

## Instant Christian themes
### for assemblies, classrooms and mid-week clubs

Text copyright © 1998 Zoë Crutchley and Veronica Parnell
Illustrations copyright © 1998 Andy Robb

The authors assert the moral right to be identified as the authors of this work

Published by
**The Bible Reading Fellowship**
Peter's Way, Sandy Lane West
Oxford OX4 5HG
ISBN 1 84101 003 0

First edition 1998
10 9 8 7 6 5 4 3 2 1 0

**Acknowledgments**
Unless otherwise indicated, scriptures are quoted from the *Good News Bible*
published by The Bible Societies/HarperCollins*Publishers* Ltd UK
© American Bible Society, 1966, 1971, 1976, 1992.
*Contemporary English Version* © American Bible Society, 1991, 1992, 1995.

A catalogue record for this book is available from the British Library

Printed and bound in Malta by Interprint Ltd

# Contents

# Mathematics

## Jesus Feeds a Large Crowd . . . . . . . . . . . 17

**Bible Reference:** Mark 6:30–44

**Aim:** To introduce the concept of Jesus as a caring teacher

**National Curriculum Pointer:** Number

**Activities Focus:** Fractions and the numbers involved in the story

## Noah and the Flood . . . . . . . . . . . . . . . . 25

**Bible Reference:** Genesis 6:9–22

Genesis 7:11–14

Genesis 7:17–20

Genesis 8:1–19

Genesis 9:8–13

**Aim:** To help the children understand that God cares for us

**National Curriculum Pointer:** Number, Shape, Space and Measures

**Activities Focus:** The dimensions of the ark, and counting

## David and Goliath . . . . . . . . . . . . . . . . . 31

**Bible Reference:** 1 Samuel 17:1–17

1 Samuel 17:20–23

1 Samuel 17:32–50

**Aim:** To introduce David as a servant of God

**National Curriculum Pointer:** Shape, Space and Measures

**Key Stage One:** Using and applying mathematics

**Key Stage Two:** Handling data

**Activities Focus:** Measurement, comparison and probability

## The Covenant Box . . . . . . . . . . . . . . . . . 39

**Bible Reference:** Exodus 25:10–22

Exodus 20:1–17

**Aim:** To introduce the Ten Commandments

**National Curriculum Pointer:** Shape, Space and Measures

**Activities Focus:** Measuring

# Science

# Design & Technology

# History

# Geography

# Introduction

*Instant Inspiration* has been written to enable teachers to use a Christian assembly as either the beginning or conclusion of a particular Programme of Study within the National Curriculum. It also enables a mid-week club or children's leader to present a relevant school assembly. Although primarily a resource book for use in the context of an assembly, *Instant Inspiration* can easily be used as the basis of a mid-week club programme, or even for a Sunday group meeting.

*Instant Inspiration* contains five units with four assembly planners in each. Each unit is focused on a subject in the National Curriculum. The subjects covered are Mathematics, Science, Design and Technology, History, and Geography. Every assembly has a clear Christian aim, which is explored within part of a Programme of Study both at Key Stage One and Key Stage Two. A series of activities follows each assembly planner. The range of activities, many supported by photocopiable sheets, enables both the teacher and the mid-week club or children's leader to develop the Christian aim and the National Curriculum link that is introduced.

Every assembly planner and activities section contains the following:

## BIBLE REFERENCE

The Bible references are quoted in full from the Good News Bible, Version Two. This makes for ease of use during planning and also allows personal Bible study to become an integral part of preparation. A deep understanding of the Christian teaching will aid in interpreting its message for the children; an additional Bible reading guide specific to the passage may also aid study. Try a local Christian bookshop for suggestions of suitable materials; alternatively, contact The Bible Reading Fellowship, Peter's Way, Sandy Lane West, Oxford, OX4 5HG; Tel: 01865 748227.

## NATIONAL CURRICULUM POINTER

The National Curriculum pointer shows the primary educational focus of both the assembly planner and the activities which follow.

## RESOURCES

Where appropriate, each section has a resources list which gives an overview of the materials needed to carry through the activty.

## AIM

The aim is a guide to the biblically based Christian teaching involved.

## INTRODUCTION

The introduction provides a lead into the theme of the assembly, giving the children a chance to settle down and begin to listen attentively. This is particularly useful in an assembly situation or for a mid-week club or children's leader using it to move the club from activity to Christian teaching.

## STORY

The story is the 'heart' of each assembly planner, but could also be used as a quiet, thoughtful pause in a busy mid-week club. The stories are told in many ways, from a simple tale illustrated by OHP pictures, to a puppet play. There are opportunities within the telling of the stories to involve the children in active participation, thus maintaining their interest and allowing the teaching point to be conveyed quickly and easily.

## PRAYERS

The prayers focus on the Christian aim, but have been written to capture the children's imagination. There are some that require a response, others that encourage the children to think; but all are firmly rooted in the Christian teaching of the particular assembly theme.

## ACTIVITIES

A set of activities follows each assembly planner. Although there is a wide diversity, all are focused on the biblical base and the National Curriculum pointer. Within *Instant Inspiration* there are:

### Games

The variety of games has been carefully planned so that some can be used with a large group, others with a small group and yet others with pairs of children working together. Space has also been taken into consideration, so there are games that can be played in open spaces and games that can be played simply on a tabletop. There are active and quiet games, but they all enable the children to learn whilst having fun.

### Art and craft

These activities range from simple cutting out and colouring activities to larger collages and 3D model making.

### Pencil activities

Pencil activities often encompass school-based skills and at first sight may appear to be more suitable for use in the classroom, where they will provide opportunities for solid teaching, the practice of skills and assessment of individual progress. However, for a mid-week club or children's leader who wants to make their Christian teaching relevant to the children's school life, they will be useful.

## Food

Food-based activities are always popular, particularly when there is a chance to taste the final results! It is important that food handling and kitchen safety rules are both taught and carefully observed during these activities. Remember to be aware of food allergies.

## Music

Music occurs within the activities although it has not been included in the assembly planners. This is because every situation calls for a different style of music and many people have their own favourites. If music is an important part of the assembly format, some of the music activities can easily be adapted for use. Alternatively, hymns, songs and musical accompaniments relevant to the children and the teaching point involved can be found.

## Extension activity

An extension activity allows a particular topic or point of interest to be extended into a long-term project, allowing the children to spend time exploring it in greater depth and detail.

## PHOTOCOPIABLE SHEETS

These are used in a number of ways within *Instant Inspiration*. Some are used as illustrations for the story, some as a focus for prayers, others have been carefully designed to provide activities of differing lengths. Therefore, some will appeal to younger children (Key Stage One) whilst others will happily occupy an older child (Key Stage Two). Many of the photocopiable sheets provide a self-contained activity, cutting down on preparation time; as such they also have value as Take Home Sheets, enabling the children to share their learning experiences within their home environment.

## TIPS FOR ADAPTING INSTANT INSPIRATION FOR A MID-WEEK CLUB

◆ *Change the* Instant Inspiration *format to your meeting pattern*

◆ *If necessary, play the games as individuals, not teams*

◆ *Make sure that you 'mix and match' activities for a balanced meeting*

◆ *Be aware that the relationship between a mid-week club or children's leader and a child is different from that between a pupil and teacher. Change the language of* Instant Inspiration *if you need to*

## TIPS FOR PRESENTING AN ASSEMBLY

◆ *Read the assembly planner carefully; become familiar with its contents*

◆ *Try to engender a worshipful atmosphere*

◆ *Make sure that everyone can hear you*

◆ *If possible, make sure that everybody can see you*

◆ *Try to look around at the children and establish eye contact*

◆ *Try to learn the majority of the story*

◆ *Control the pace*

◆ *Don't be afraid to pause to create excitement or highlight a specific point*

◆ *Don't be boring—*
*change your tone and facial expression to give different emphasis*

◆ *Don't be afraid to wait for silence before leading into quieter moments*

◆ *If you are a mid-week club or children's leader,*
*liaise closely with the school*

## THINKING ABOUT CHILD SAFETY

Alongside the things you should check when running a group, such as the details of the Children Act, insurance cover, health and safety rules and fire regulations, one of the most important factors to be aware of is whether your church already has a Policy for protecting the children in your care. If your church has such a Policy you need to make sure that you are fully conversant with its contents. If your church does not have such a Policy, one or all of the following may be able to help:

*Your local diocese*

*Your local authority*

*Churches' Child Protection*
*Advisory Service (PCCA Child Care)*
*PO Box 133*
*Swanley*
*Kent*
*BR8 7UQ*

*Kids' Clubs Network*
*Bellerive House*
*3, Muirfield Crescent*
*London*
*E14 9SZ*

*The Baptist Union of Great Britain*
*Baptist House*
*PO Box 444*
*129, Broadway*
*Didcot*
*Oxfordshire*
*OX11 8RT*

*Instant Inspiration* offers a wealth of resources to both the primary school teacher and the mid-week club or children's leader. Pick an assembly and be inspired *NOW*!

Mathematics

# Jesus Feeds a Large Crowd

## Mark 6:30–44

The apostles returned and met with Jesus, and told him all they had done and taught. There were so many people coming and going that Jesus and his disciples didn't even have time to eat. So he said to them, 'Let us go off by ourselves to some place where we will be alone and you can rest for a while.' So they started out in a boat by themselves for a lonely place.

Many people, however, saw them leave and knew at once who they were; so they went from all the towns and ran ahead by land and arrived at the place ahead of Jesus and his disciples. When Jesus got out of the boat, he saw this large crowd, and his heart was filled with pity for them, because they were like sheep without a shepherd. So he began to teach them many things. When it was getting late, his disciples came to him and said, 'It is already very late, and this is a lonely place. Send the people away, and let them go to the nearby farms and villages in order to buy themselves something to eat.'

'You yourselves give them something to eat,' Jesus answered.

They asked, 'Do you want us to go and spend two hundred silver coins on bread in order to feed them?'

So Jesus asked them, 'How much bread have you got? Go and see.'

When they found out, they told him, 'Five loaves and also two fish.'

Jesus then told his disciples to make all the people divide into groups and sit down on the green grass. So the people sat down in rows, in groups of a hundred and groups of fifty. Then Jesus took the five loaves and the two fish, looked up to heaven, and gave thanks to God. He broke the loaves and gave them to his disciples to distribute to the people. He also divided the two fish among them all. Everyone ate and had enough. Then the disciples took up twelve baskets full of what was left of the bread and the fish. The number of men who were fed was five thousand.

## NATIONAL CURRICULUM POINTER: NUMBER

### INTRODUCTION

**RESOURCES:** five bread rolls and two cut-outs of a fish or two tins of tuna/ sardines/salmon, etc; plate

Show the children the bread and fish. Discuss school dinners—it might be sandwiches, it may be a cooked meal. Ask them if they think you have enough food to provide a school dinner for everybody in the room. You should get the answer, 'No, there's not enough.' Tell the children that in the Bible there is a story where Jesus has the same amount of food that you have just shown them, but Jesus had to feed five thousand people.

### AIM: To introduce the concept of Jesus as a caring teacher

### STORY

**RESOURCES:** photocopiable sheet (Story) turned into four separate OHP slides

*Tell the following story, displaying the relevant OHP slide at the appropriate point. It is important to leave the slides in place so that the children can see four separate slides turning into one whole picture.*

One day Jesus and his disciples were particularly tired, so Jesus suggested that they all go in a small boat to a quiet place on the other side of the lake, away from the crowds. Jesus and his disciples got into the boat and set off across the lake. When they landed they were very surprised to find that the people they had left behind had in fact walked around the lake shore to meet them. *(Show OHP 1.)* Jesus felt sorry for all the people who were so keen to learn all he could teach them and, even though he was exhausted, he started to talk to them about his Father God.

The crowd listened eagerly to Jesus for a long time. The disciples were growing more and more tired and hungry. They went to Jesus and said 'Isn't it time you sent these people home? Everyone needs something to eat and there is nowhere here for them to buy food.' *(Show OHP 2.)* Jesus told his disciples that they should feed the people themselves. The disciples said, 'We haven't enough money. We would need two hundred silver coins.' Jesus looked at his disciples and asked, 'What food have we got amongst us?' The disciples went to find out. Some time later they came back to Jesus and said, 'All we can find is five small loaves and two fish'. *(Show OHP 3.)*

Jesus surprised his disciples by saying to the people, 'Sit down in groups and rows and we will bring you something to eat.' The disciples found it hard to believe that Jesus could feed five thousand people with the small amount of food they had found. They watched as Jesus took the loaves and the fish, thanked God, and shared the food out to them. He told the disciples to distribute the food to the people, and make sure that everybody had enough to eat. *(Show OHP 4.)* After everybody had had plenty to eat, the disciples went round to tidy up and collect the leftovers. They were amazed to find that they could fill twelve baskets with the left over food.

*Many Christians like this story because it shows a picture of Jesus as a kind and caring teacher. You could ask the children if they can suggest points from the story which show Jesus being kind and caring.*

*Before you move on to prayers you might like to point out to the children that you used four OHP pictures which together made one whole story. Ask if any of the children can tell you the special name for one of these four parts of a whole.*

## PRAYERS

Tell the children to be very quiet and still as you focus your collective thoughts towards God. Use one or both of the following prayers.

---

**Dear God,**
**Thank you for the story we have just heard.**
**Help us to remember people who have not got enough to eat—**
    **children who go to sleep at night hungry;**
        **mothers who don't eat in order to feed their babies.**
**Thank you that we all have plenty to eat.**
**Help us to remember the way Jesus showed his care for the people**
    **by feeding them with bread and fish.**
**Show us ways in which we can help the hungry. Amen**

---

You may like to follow up this prayer by planning an event to raise money for a charity which feeds hungry people.

### An Acrostic Prayer

Explain to the children that you are going to say an acrostic prayer, where the first letter in every line will be one letter of the word 'bread'. You might like to illustrate this point with cut-out letters or an OHP slide.

    **B** near us.
    **R** emind us of your love.
    **E** ternal Father,
    **A** ll the days of our life,
    **D** raw closer to us. Amen

You could suggest to the children that they try to write their own acrostic prayer using the word 'fish'.

Follow up this assembly, enabling the children to practise mathematical skills by using the most appropriate activities for your group from the selection below.

## ACTIVITIES

### Colour a Fraction

**RESOURCES:**
photocopiable sheet (Fractions); pencils; crayons; felt-tips

Give each child a copy of the photocopiable sheet (Fractions) and remind them of the story. Point out that they have a picture of the five small loaves and the two fish that Jesus used to feed five thousand people. Ask the children to look at

the first loaf and draw a line through it, which will split the loaf into two halves. Then tell the children to colour in one half of the loaf. The children could write both the symbol and the word 'half' by the side of the loaf. Continue in this way, asking the children to colour in a half, a quarter or a whole of each remaining item. If you are using this sheet with older children (Key Stage Two) you might like to tell them to colour in a percentage of each item, or a more complex fraction.

## Make a Number Game

**RESOURCES:** a badge for each child (you could use sticky labels) showing either a fraction or a whole number; tokens such as clean milk bottle tops optional)

Take the children to a large open space where you can play the game in safety. Give each child their badge and explain that they are going to run around the space wearing their badge. Exercise care when making or buying the badges to ensure that they are safe for use in this situation. Tell the children that you will say a number or a fraction. When the children hear what you say, they must get into groups so that their badges make up the

number or fraction you have said. For instance, if you say, 'One and a half' the children must get into groups so that their badges total one and a half. The group could be made up of three children, each with a badge showing a half; or it could be two children, one with a badge showing one and the other with a badge showing a half. After the children have got into groups and you have checked that they have done this correctly, make sure that the children split up again and run around until you announce the next number. If you want to make the game competitive you could give a token to each member of the first group to get together correctly after you have announced a number. The winner would then be the child with the most tokens at the end of the game.

## Share a Sandwich

**RESOURCES:** bread; butter or spread; a fish filling—you could use fish paste or tinned fish; plates; knives

As this is an activity involving food and food preparation, make sure that everybody understands and obeys kitchen safety and food hygiene rules throughout it. When selecting the bread to use, you will need to choose a loaf that will give you square slices of bread. Remind the children of the story in which Jesus cared for the people by feeding them with loaves and fish. Give each child a plate and a knife and supervise carefully as they each make their own fish sandwich. The sandwiches should be made as normal, with two buttered slices of bread and a filling between them. Once each child has made a sandwich, go on to give the children a series of instructions such as, 'Carefully cut a quarter out of your sandwich and give it to the person sitting next to you'; 'Give twenty-five per cent of your sandwich to the person opposite you'; 'give a third of your remaining sandwich to your friend', and so on. When every child has given away all of their sandwich they should all still have enough to eat. Say a simple Grace and share the sandwiches together, remembering the story of the loaves and fishes.

## Find the Baskets Game

**RESOURCES:** cut-out basket shapes (twelve for each child); tokens, such as clean milk bottle tops

Before this activity, make your cut-out basket shapes from thin card or paper, then hide them around the playing area. Make sure that this area is large enough for you to play the game safely. When you are ready to play the game, remind the children of the story in which Jesus fed the large crowd. Ask if they can remember how many fish and loaves were used and how many baskets of leftovers the disciples collected. Tell the children that it is important for them to remember that there were twelve baskets of leftovers, because they are going to play a game in which they have to try to find the baskets. Explain that there are cut-out baskets hidden around the playing area. Tell the children that you will ask for a certain number of baskets and the first child to bring the correct number of cut-out baskets to you will be given a token. The winner will be the child with the most tokens at the end of the game. Tell the children to spread out; then say, 'Bring me half of the disciples' baskets'. They should each bring you six. You could then go on to ask for 'a quarter of the baskets' or 'seventy-five per cent of the baskets', and so on. At the end of the game, point out to the children that Jesus did not just give the crowd a little to eat, he gave them more than they needed and there were leftovers.

## Missing Words

**RESOURCES:** photocopiable sheet (Missing Words); pencils; crayons or felt-tips; Bibles for reference

Give each child a copy of the photocopiable sheet (Missing Words), and explain that some of the words in the story are missing. For younger children (Key Stage One) read the sheet through, with the children putting in the missing words verbally as you go. Tell the children to try to complete the sheet for themselves. Older children (Key Stage Two) could complete the sheet on their own, referring to the Bible when necessary. When the missing words have been filled in, the children could go on to colour in the pictures around the text.

## Collage of the Five Loaves and Two Fish

**RESOURCES:** collage materials; glue; scissors; paper; card; pencils; pictures that show different artistic representations of the loaves and fish (for instance, mosaics, embroidered banners, etc.)

Ask the children if they can remember how many loaves and how many fish Jesus used to feed how many people. Show the children the pictures of the loaves and fish that you have collected and ask them to design their own picture that they will collage later. Discuss the different designs, making sure that each contains two fish and five loaves. When the designs are complete, explain that the children will collage their designs but they must make sure that they follow your instructions carefully. Give the children instructions, such as:

*Collage one fish half green and half blue.*

*Collage one fish a quarter yellow and three quarters red.*

*Collage one loaf twenty-five per cent brown and seventy-five per cent white.*

*Collage two loaves yellow.*

*Collage half the remaining loaves brown and the other half gold.*

Make sure that the instructions you give are appropriate for the children in your group. You could divide the children into small groups and give each group separate instructions or, if you only have a few children, you could give each child separate instructions. When the collages are complete you might like to use them to make an eye-catching wall display entitled 'Jesus the Caring Teacher'.

The boat by the shore

1

The crowd eating

4

Jesus and the disciples

2

The disciples find the loaves and fish

3

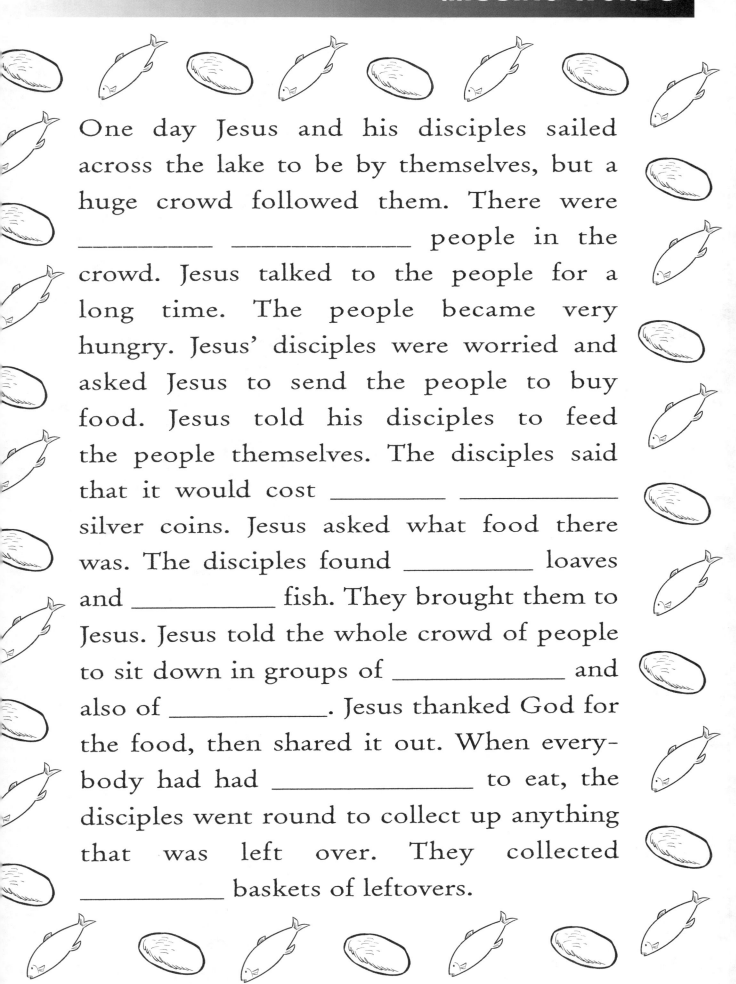

One day Jesus and his disciples sailed across the lake to be by themselves, but a huge crowd followed them. There were _____ _____ people in the crowd. Jesus talked to the people for a long time. The people became very hungry. Jesus' disciples were worried and asked Jesus to send the people to buy food. Jesus told his disciples to feed the people themselves. The disciples said that it would cost _____ _____ silver coins. Jesus asked what food there was. The disciples found _____ loaves and _____ fish. They brought them to Jesus. Jesus told the whole crowd of people to sit down in groups of _____ and also of _____. Jesus thanked God for the food, then shared it out. When everybody had had _____ to eat, the disciples went round to collect up anything that was left over. They collected _____ baskets of leftovers.

# Noah and the Flood

## Genesis 6:9–22

This is the story of Noah. He had three sons, Shem, Ham, and Japheth. Noah had no faults and was the only good man of his time. He lived in fellowship with God, but everyone else was evil in God's sight, and violence had spread everywhere. God looked at the world and saw that it was evil, for the people were all living evil lives.

God said to Noah, 'I have decided to put an end to the whole human race. I will destroy them completely, because the world is full of their violent deeds. Build a boat for yourself out of good timber; make rooms in it and cover it with tar inside and out. Make it 133 metres long, 22 metres wide, and 13 metres high. Make a roof for the boat and leave a space of 44 centimetres between the roof and the sides. Build it with three decks and put a door in the side. I am going to send a flood on the earth to destroy every living being. Everything on the earth will die, but I will make a covenant with you. Go into the boat with your wife, your sons, and their wives. Take into the boat with you a male and a female of every kind of animal and of every kind of bird, in order to keep them alive. Take along all kinds of food for you and for them.' Noah did everything that God commanded.

## Genesis 7:11–14

When Noah was six hundred years old, on the seventeenth day of the second month all the outlets of the vast body of water beneath the earth burst open, all the floodgates of the sky were opened, and rain fell on the earth for forty days and nights. On that same day Noah and his wife went into the boat with their three sons, Shem, Ham, and Japheth, and their wives. With them went every kind of animal, domestic and wild, large and small, and every kind of bird.

## Genesis 7:17–20

The flood continued for forty days, and the water became deep enough for the boat to float. The water became deeper, and the boat drifted on the surface. It became so deep that it covered the highest mountains; it went on rising until it was about seven metres above the tops of the mountains.

## Genesis 8:1–19

God had not forgotten Noah and all the animals with him in the boat; he caused a wind to blow, and the water started going down. The outlets of the water beneath the earth and the floodgates of the sky were closed. The rain stopped, and the water gradually went down for a hundred and fifty days. On the seventeenth day of the seventh month the boat came to rest on a mountain in the Ararat range. The water kept going down, and on the first day of the tenth month the tops of the mountains appeared.

After forty days Noah opened a window and sent out a raven. It did not come back, but kept flying around until the water was completely gone. Meanwhile, Noah sent out a dove to see if the water had gone down, but since the water covered all the land, the dove did not find a place to alight. It flew back to the boat, and Noah reached out and took it in. He waited another seven days and sent out the dove again. It returned to him in the evening with a fresh olive leaf in its beak. So Noah knew that the water had gone down. Then he waited another seven days and sent out the dove once more; this time it did not come back.

When Noah was 601 years old, on the first day of the first month, the water was gone. Noah removed the covering of the boat, looked round, and saw that the ground was getting dry. By the twenty-seventh day of the second month the earth was completely dry.

God said to Noah, 'Go out of the boat with your wife, your sons, and their wives. Take all the birds and animals out with you, so that they may reproduce and spread over all the earth.' So Noah went out of the boat with his wife, his sons, and their wives. All the animals and birds went out of the boat in groups of their own kind.

## Genesis 9:8–13

God said to Noah and his sons, 'I am now making my covenant with you and with your descendants, and with all living beings—all birds and all animals—everything that came out of the boat with you. With these words I make my covenant with you: I promise that never again will all living beings be destroyed by a flood; never again will a flood destroy the earth. As a sign of this everlasting covenant which I am making with you and with all living beings, I am putting my bow in the clouds. It will be the sign of my covenant with the world.'

## INTRODUCTION

### RESOURCES:

Wet-weather outfit for yourself, including umbrella and wellingtons

Lead the assembly in your wet-weather outfit. Ask the children what sort of weather they think you are expecting. Hopefully they will say 'rain'! Ask the children how long they think it might rain for. Ask them if they think the rain will stop. Ask if anybody knows what you can sometimes see when the rain is stopping and the sun begins to shine. They should answer, 'A rainbow.' Go on to explain that in the Bible there is a story in which the rain doesn't stop for forty days and forty nights.

## AIM: To help the children understand that God cares for us

## STORY

*Give each year group or class or individual child an animal name and appropriate sound. You will need lions (roar), elephants (trumpet), snakes (hiss), bees (buzz), dogs (bark), crocodiles (snap), horses (neigh), cows (moo), doves (coo) and ravens (caw). Let the groups practise their sounds together for a few moments only! Explain that, when the name of their animal is mentioned in the story, they must make their animal sound just twice. Tell the following story, pausing for the children to make their animal sounds at the points indicated.*

Long, long ago, everybody in the world was very wicked, except for one man whose name was Noah. Noah was a friend of God and often talked to him. One day God told Noah that because everybody in the world was very wicked he had decided to destroy the living creatures in the world with a great flood; but because Noah was his friend, God wanted him to build a big boat. God told Noah how to build the boat and what size it must be. God also told him that when the boat was finished he must go on board with his wife, his sons and their wives. But before they went on board they must put on to the boat two of every living bird, animal and insect. Noah was

very surprised. 'How can I put an **elephant** with a **lion**? Or a **snake** with a **bee**? Won't the **crocodile** eat the **dog**?' he asked his wife. She smiled and said, 'Just you build the boat and trust God.'

Noah and his three sons worked very hard and finished the huge boat, even though people laughed at them. The boat was very big. It was 133 metres long and 22 metres wide. At last God said to Noah, 'Get into the boat with your family and the animals.' Two **elephants** walked into the boat, swinging their trunks as they went. The **elephants** were followed by two fierce **lions**. In the air above the **lions** flew two **bees**. The **bees** zoomed into the boat ahead of the **snakes**, who had to slither up the gangplank. The **snakes** reached the deck and coiled themselves into a cosy, dark corner just as two **doves** flew in through the window. The **doves** were followed by two black **ravens**, who perched in the rafters of the cabin roof. The **dogs** were very excited as they ran up the gangplank and barked loudly at the **crocodiles**. Noah had some difficulty in persuading the **cows** to leave the juicy grass and go up the gangplank but eventually he managed to coax them inside the boat. The **horses** were very keen to get on board and trotted up the gangplank eagerly.

Once all the living creatures were on board, Noah checked the list of food and settled down to wait. That same day God shut the door of the boat behind Noah, his family and all the living creatures, and it began to rain. It rained for forty days and nights. Soon the boat was lifted up by the water and floated away. It rained and it rained and it rained! Eventually the rain stopped and the water gradually went down. As the water went down, the boat came to rest on the top of a mountain.

After forty days, Noah sent out a **raven**. Noah was hoping the **raven** would find dry land and come back to let him know, but the **raven** never returned. Noah waited for a week and then sent out a **dove** to see if the water had gone down. The **dove** could not find anywhere to perch so it came back to Noah. Another week went by and Noah decided to try again. He sent the **dove** out again and this time it came back with a green leaf in its beak. At last God told Noah to leave the boat with his family and all the living creatures. The **horses** were the first to leave the boat, closely followed by the **cows**, who were anxious to eat fresh green grass again. The **dogs** ran off, barking happily. The **crocodiles** walked sedately down the gangplank. Noah watched until all the animals had safely left the boat. God said to Noah, 'I will put a rainbow in the sky as a sign that I promise that never again will all living creatures be destroyed by a great flood.'

*At the end of the story, remind the children that when they see a rainbow they should remember the story they have heard and the promise God made to Noah.*

## PRAYERS

## Animal Prayer

Tell the children that when you mention their animal in the prayer they should make the animal noises just twice, as they did in the story.

**Dear God,**
**Thank you for all living creatures,**
  **from the great big elephant to the tiny bee.**
**Thank you for the white wings of doves against a blue sky.**
**Thank you for ravens that soar overhead.**
**Thank you for the different sounds animals make**
  **—the roar of the lion and the hiss of the snake.**
**Thank you for animals that live alongside us and work with us**
  **—the dog and the horse.**
**Thank you for animals that give us food,**
  **like the cow who gives us milk.**
**Thank you for wild animals like the crocodiles**
  **who lurk in distant rivers.**
**Thank you for everything that shares the world with us.**
**Help us to look after them. Amen**

## A Water Prayer

**RESOURCES:** a bowl of water (a washing-up bowl is ideal); a jug; water

Tell the children to shut their eyes and listen to the sounds that water makes. While the children sit quietly with their eyes closed, pour some water from the jug into the bowl. Do this several times. As they listen they should try to think about all the uses that we have for clean, fresh water. They could think about cooling drinks on a hot day, refreshing showers or the fun they have when they go swimming. After a few moments' silence, say the following sentence of prayer to bring the time of reflection to a close.

**Thank you, God, for**
**clean, fresh water. Amen**

Follow up this assembly, enabling the children to practise mathematical skills by using the most appropriate activities for your group from the selection suggested.

## ACTIVITIES

## Animals and the Ark

**RESOURCES:** photocopiable sheet (Ark); pencils; crayons; felt-tips

Give each child a copy of the photocopiable sheet (Ark). Discuss the story with the children, reminding them that the rainbow is God's promise to the world. Talk about the things on the sheet and the missing numbers. Tell the children to complete the missing numbers by themselves. When the sheets are complete and you have checked that the numbers the children have filled in are correct, tell the children to colour in the picture carefully. For older children you might like to ask them to write their version of the story. This, together with their coloured-in sheet, could be displayed on the wall or in a booklet.

## Living Creatures Search

**RESOURCES:** photocopiable sheet (Living Creatures); pencils; crayons; scissors; thin card; glue; sticky-back plastic; tokens

This photocopiable sheet can be used in a variety of ways:

**1)** Give each child a copy of the photocopiable sheet (Living Creatures). Explain that the sheet shows just some of the creatures that Noah took into the boat with him and his family. Tell the children to count how many of each sort of creature there are on the sheet and join the matching creatures together with different coloured lines. For instance, you might join all the lions together with an orange line.

**2)** Give each child a copy of the photocopiable sheet (Living Creatures). Tell the children to colour in, then cut out, two of each kind of creature. The creatures should be stuck on to thin card and then cut out to make playing cards. If you want to make the cards more durable, they could be covered with sticky-back plastic. The children can play a game with these cards by spreading all of them out face down, then taking it in turns to turn over two cards. If the cards turned over are the same, the child may keep that pair and have another turn. If the cards turned over are different, the cards must be replaced face down and another child takes their turn. At the end of the game the children could count up their cards in groups of two, three or maybe four. The winner is the child with the most cards.

**3)** If you make up cards as in 2) above but using a number of photocopiable sheets (Living Creatures) you can use the cards to play a 'search' game. Before playing the game hide the cards around your playing area. (Make sure that you have enough space to play the game safely.) Tell the children that you will ask them to look for a certain number of each creature and the child who brings them to you first will receive a token. The winner of the game will be the child with the most tokens at the end of play. Start the game by giving instructions such as, 'Find me two goats,' or, 'Find me three lions,' and so on. For older children you could tell them how many of each type of creature you have hidden around the playing area, then ask them to find 'fifty per cent of the rhinos' and so on.

## Noah's Walk

**RESOURCES:** dimensions of the boat displayed where the children can see them easily; stopwatches; paper; pencils; calculators (optional); metre sticks or tape-measures

Before the activity, write the dimensions of Noah's boat clearly on a poster-sized piece of paper or something similar. Divide the children into pairs; tell each pair to experiment and discover how long it takes them to walk one metre. Then tell them to calculate how long it would take to walk the length of Noah's boat. The children could then go on to calculate how long it would take to walk the length and back. Tell the children to discuss between themselves how many times Noah might have had to walk up and down the boat each day. Remind them of the story about how God told Noah to take two of each creature on to the boat to save them from destruction in the flood, and how Noah trusted God and did as he was told. Explain that Noah presumably had to feed the creatures every day and clean them out too. This must have involved a lot of walking. The children could go on to calculate how far Noah would have walked during the forty days and nights of rain.

## How Much Room?

**RESOURCES:** pencils; paper; calculators (optional); books on keeping a pet (for reference)

Discuss the story with the children, thinking about how big the boat was that God asked Noah to build. Talk about keeping animals. Noah had a large number of animals to look after and keep healthy. Tell the children that one of the first decisions you have to make, when thinking about keeping a pet, is how much space it needs and whether you have that amount of room in your home or garden. Explain that there are several ways to work out how much space a certain creature needs. For instance, explain that if you want to keep fish, they are kept in a tank called an aquarium. It is important to know how many fish you can keep in one tank, particularly if your tank has an unusual shape. Many books on keeping fish will tell you how to work out how many fish you can keep in a certain sized tank. In the same way, books about keeping small animals such as rabbits or hamsters explain how to work out what size living conditions the animals need. Tell the children to choose a pet they might like to keep. Then, using the resource books, tell the children to estimate how big the animal would be when fully grown. The children can then go on to calculate how big the living quarters of their chosen pet would need to be. You could go on to draw the proposed living quarters to scale.

## ✚ EXTENSION ACTIVITY

**RESOURCES:** chalk; an enormous space; tape-measures

If you have enough space, try to measure out the dimensions of the boat. It really is a lot bigger than the children will expect. You could measure it in both metric and imperial units. You could mark out the boat by using chalk or skipping-ropes to give you an idea of the size.

**ARK**

There are _____ animals in the picture.

The animals in the picture have a total of _____ legs.

There are _____ windows in the boat.

There are _____ people in the picture.

There are _____ birds in the picture.

There are _____ insects in the picture.

# David and Goliath

## 1 Samuel 17:1–17

The Philistines gathered for battle in Socoh, a town in Judah; they camped at a place called Ephes Dammim, between Socoh and Azekah. Saul and the Israelites assembled and camped in the Valley of Elah, where they got ready to fight the Philistines. The Philistines lined up on one hill and the Israelites on another, with a valley between them.

A man named Goliath, from the city of Gath, came out from the Philistine camp to challenge the Israelites. He was nearly three metres tall and wore bronze armour that weighed about fifty-seven kilogrammes and a bronze helmet. His legs were also protected by bronze armour, and he carried a bronze javelin slung over his shoulder. His spear was as thick as the bar on a weaver's loom, and its iron head weighed about seven kilogrammes. A soldier walked in front of him carrying his shield. Goliath stood and shouted at the Israelites, 'What are you doing there, lined up for battle? I am a Philistine, you slaves of Saul! Choose one of your men to fight me. If he wins and kills me, we will be your slaves; but if I win and kill him, you will be our slaves. Here and now I challenge the Israelite army. I dare you to pick someone to fight me!' When Saul and his men heard this, they were terrified.

David was the son of Jesse, who was an Ephrathite from Bethlehem in Judah. Jesse had eight sons, and at the time Saul was king, he was already a very old man. His three eldest sons had gone with Saul to war. The eldest was Eliab, the next was Abinadab, and the third was Shammah. David was the youngest son, and while the three eldest brothers stayed with Saul, David would go back to Bethlehem from time to time, to take care of his father's sheep.

Goliath challenged the Israelites every morning and evening for forty days.

One day Jesse said to David, 'Take ten kilogrammes of this roasted grain and these ten loaves of bread, and hurry with them to your brothers in the camp.'

## 1 Samuel 17:20–23

David got up early the next morning, left someone else in charge of the sheep, took the food, and went as Jesse had told him to. He arrived at the camp just as the Israelites were going out to their battle line, shouting the war-cry. The Philistine and the Israelite armies took up positions for battle, facing each other. David left the food with the officer in charge of the supplies, ran to the battle line, went to his brothers, and asked how they were getting on. As he was talking to them, Goliath came forward and challenged the Israelites as he had done before. And David heard him.

## 1 Samuel 17:32–50

David said to Saul, 'Your Majesty, no one should be afraid of this Philistine! I will go and fight him.'

'No,' answered Saul. 'How could you fight him? You're just a boy and he has been a soldier all his life!'

'Your Majesty,' David said, 'I take care of my father's sheep. Whenever a lion or a bear carries off a lamb, I go after it, attack it, and rescue the lamb. And if the lion or bear turns on me, I grab it by the throat and beat it to death. I have killed lions and bears, and I will do the same to this heathen Philistine, who has defied the army of the living God. The Lord has saved me from lions and bears; he will save me from this Philistine.'

'All right,' Saul answered. 'Go, and the Lord be with you.' He gave his own armour to David for him to wear: a bronze helmet, which he put on David's head, and a coat of armour. David strapped Saul's sword over the armour and tried to walk, but he couldn't, because he wasn't used to wearing them. 'I can't fight with all this,' he said to Saul. 'I'm not used to it.' So he took it all off. He took his shepherd's stick and then picked up five smooth stones from the stream and put them in his bag. With his sling ready, he went out to meet Goliath.

The Philistine started walking towards David, with his shield-bearer walking in front of him. He kept coming closer, and when he got a good look at David, he was filled with scorn for him because he was just a nice, good-looking boy. He said to David, 'What's that stick for? Do you think I'm a dog?' And he called down curses from his god on David. 'Come on,' he challenged David, 'and I will give your body to the birds and animals to eat.'

David answered, 'You are coming against me with sword, spear, and javelin, but I come against you in the name of the Lord Almighty, the God of the Israelite armies, which you have defied. This very day the Lord will put you in my power; I will defeat you and cut off your head. And I will give the bodies of the Philistine soldiers to the birds and animals to eat. Then the whole world will know that Israel has a God, and everyone here will see that the Lord does not need swords or spears to save his people. He is victorious in battle, and he will put all of you in our power.'

Goliath started walking towards David again, and David ran quickly towards the Philistine battle line to fight him. He put his hand into his bag and took out a stone, which he slung at Goliath.

It hit him on the forehead and broke his skull, and Goliath fell face downwards on the ground. And so, without a sword, David defeated and killed Goliath with a sling and a stone!

# AIM:

# To introduce David as a servant of God

## INTRODUCTION

**RESOURCES:** photocopiable sheet (Size Sequence) used as a series of OHP slides

Before the assembly, turn the photocopiable sheet (Size Sequence) into a series of OHP slides. You might prefer to use only three pictures. At the assembly, show the children the pictures and ask for a volunteer to point out the picture of the largest dog. Then ask for a volunteer to point out the picture of the smallest dog. Finally, ask for a volunteer to point out a picture of a middle-sized dog. Explain to the children that dogs come in a variety of sizes. One of the biggest dogs is a Great Dane, while some dogs, like the chihuahua, are so tiny that they could be easily carried in a small basket. Tell the children that in the Bible there is a story about a small boy and an enormous giant.

## STORY

**RESOURCES:** five soft foam balls numbered 1 to 5; five volunteers; five scripts

*Before the assembly, ask five adults to volunteer to help you tell the story of David and Goliath. If it is not possible to find five adults, choose five sensible, older children from your group. Give each volunteer a script which they will read aloud when you throw them one of the soft foam balls to catch. Tell the volunteers that when they have finished reading their script they must throw the ball back to you, so that you can continue the story.*

*To tell the story, show the children the five soft foam balls. Explain that, in the Bible story, a shepherd boy called David used five smooth stones, so you are going to tell them a story about David and Goliath, and instead of smooth stones you will use soft foam balls (stress the safety reasons for this).*

NARRATOR: The army of Israel was fighting a war against the Philistines. Many men had joined the army of Israel and left their normal work. Three brothers who had done this were Eliab, Abinadab and Shammah. Their younger brother David was the one who had been left at home to look after the family's flock of sheep and to do any other jobs his father Jesse found for him. One day Jesse said to David:

*(Throw ball number 1 to volunteer number 1.)*

SCRIPT ONE: 'Take this food and these ten loaves of bread to your three brothers who are in the army camp. You can also take these ten cheeses and give them to your brothers' commanding officer. David, I want you to find out how your brothers are and how the war against the Philistines is progressing.'

*(Volunteer throws ball back to narrator.)*

NARRATOR: The very next morning, as soon as David woke up, he took the food and went to the army camp just like Jesse had told him. When he arrived at the camp, David gave the food to the soldier in charge of the rations and then went to find his brothers. David found his brothers and had started to chat to them when, suddenly, there was a terrific commotion in the distance on the other side of the valley. David knew that this was where the Philistines were camped.

*(Throw ball number 2 to volunteer number 2.)*

SCRIPT TWO: Every day, a giant called Goliath came out from the Philistine camp and shouted at the Israelite army, 'One of you, come and fight me. If you win, all the Philistines will be your slaves, but if I win, all of you will be our slaves.' Goliath was huge—he was nearly three metres tall. He wore impressive bronze armour and his shield-bearer walked in front of him. Goliath himself carried a spear and wore a javelin slung over his shoulder.

*(Volunteer throws ball back to narrator.)*

NARRATOR: Every time Goliath came out and shouted, the Israelite army was terrified. Nobody was brave enough to fight Goliath, even though King Saul had offered a huge reward for any man who killed the giant. David couldn't understand why nobody was willing to try and fight Goliath. He even asked his brothers about it. Some of the other soldiers heard what David was saying and told King Saul. King Saul sent for David and said:

*(Throw ball number 3 to volunteer number 3.)*

SCRIPT THREE: 'I hear you think that you can fight the giant Goliath. How can you? You are only a boy and Goliath is a giant of a man who has been a soldier for many years.' David said, 'My job at home is to guard the family's sheep. I have to protect them against lions and bears. I often killed wild animals and I will kill Goliath. The Lord will look after me when I go into battle against the giant.' King Saul agreed to let David fight Goliath and he lent David his own suit of armour.

*(Volunteer throws ball back to narrator.)*

NARRATOR: David tried to walk in the heavy suit of armour but he could not move. The armour was much too heavy for him, so he took it all off. David decided to fight the giant his own way.

*(Throw ball number 4 to volunteer number 4.)*

SCRIPT FOUR: David walked down to the stream that ran along the bottom of the valley between the two opposing army camps. He picked up five smooth stones and put them safely in the bag he carried. Then, armed only with his shepherd's sling, David set off to fight Goliath. When Goliath saw David he said:

*(Volunteer throws ball back to narrator.)*

NARRATOR: 'Are you laughing at me? You can't think that you, who are so small, can be a good match for me? If you come any nearer I'll kill you and give your body to the wild creatures.' David wasn't frightened and replied, 'God will look after me. You have challenged him but today he will put you in my power.' Goliath began to walk forward towards David, but David, rather than running away, ran eagerly towards the giant. When David judged he was near enough, he put his hand into his bag, pulled out a stone and, using his shepherd's sling, lobbed the stone at Goliath!

*(Throw ball number 5 to volunteer number 5.)*

SCRIPT FIVE: The stone spun through the air and hit Goliath on the forehead. The stone broke the giant's skull and he fell down dead.

*(Volunteer throws ball back to narrator.)*

NARRATOR: When the Philistines realized that their giant was dead, killed by a mere shepherd boy, they were terrified and ran away.

**Point out to the children that David wasn't frightened of the huge giant but trusted in God to look after him. David grew up to be a great servant of God. At this point you might like to suggest other stories about David that the children could read on their own.**

## PRAYERS

Tell the children to be very quiet and still as you focus your collective thoughts towards God. Use one or both of the following prayers.

**Dear God,**
**When we have a problem that seems as big as Goliath,**
 **help us to remember that you are there.**
**When we feel as small as David, help us to realize**
 **that with your help we can make a difference for you.**
**When we feel that the things we offer are small and inadequate like**
 **David's stones, help us to remember that you can use whatever**
 **we have, however small, to achieve your plans. Amen**

**Dear God,**
**David was your servant and all through his life he tried to follow you.**
**Even when David did something wrong he said sorry to you and you**
 **forgave him.**
**Help us to be your servants, too.**
**Help us to do the things you want us to do and remember to say**
 **sorry whenever we do something wrong. Amen**

---

Follow up this assembly, enabling the children to practise mathematical skills by using the most appropriate activities for your group from the selection below.

## ACTIVITIES

### David and Goliath Collage

**RESOURCES:** paper (long strips of wall-paper would work well); gold foil paper; glue; pencils; various collage materials; scissors

Choose the smallest child in your group and ask them to lie down on a length of wallpaper as you draw round them. Ask a tall adult to lie down on a length of wallpaper and draw round them too. Collage the smaller body shape to look like David the shepherd boy. Discuss the story with the children. What things do they think are important to add to the outline? They should mention the sling and the bag for the stones, etc. Collage the larger body shape to look like Goliath. You could read the Bible story to the children, enabling you all to check details of armour and weapons, etc. When the pictures are complete, turn them into a wall display and go on to compare the pictures of David and Goliath. Discuss height, weight and overall size.

### Fair Stone Relay?

**RESOURCES:** five scrunched-up balls of newspaper for each team; an empty cardboard box for each team; stopwatch; paper and clipboard; pencils

Take the children to a large open space where you can play the game in safety. Lay out an equally spaced line of five newspaper balls, with a cardboard box at one end. Remind the children of the five smooth stones David collected from the stream and how, with God's help, one of them killed the giant Goliath. Tell the children that you are going to time how long it takes for each of them to run and collect one ball at a time and put it in the cardboard box. They must collect all five balls. If you have a large group of children you may find it easier to divide the children into teams and let them time each other. When the timings are complete, tell the children that you are going to put the fastest children in one team and the slowest in another. Lay out two courses and make it a race. This time the first child collects the balls and the second lays the balls back out, the third collects them and so on. The winning team is the first team to complete the course. At the end of the game, discuss the result with the children. Was the result what they expected? Do they think that this was a fair race? Can the children think of any way to make it a fair race? The children might suggest that the teams are mixed up with equal numbers of fast and slow in each team. Try the race again. Is the result different?

## Size Sequence

**RESOURCES:** photocopiable sheets (Size Sequence); glue; scissors; felt-tips; crayons; paper; pencils

Tell the children that you want them to line up in size order, with the tallest at the back and the shortest at the front. When the line is complete, ask the tallest and the shortest child to remain standing while everyone else sits down. Measure the difference in height between the two children and then compare this and their individual heights with Goliath's height. You could make a height chart for the wall which records every child's height, yours and Goliath's. Give every child a copy of the photocopiable sheets (Size Sequence). Tell the children that this sheet shows a number of pictures of dogs. Emphasize that dogs can be very big (for instance, an Irish wolfhound or Great Dane) medium-sized (for instance, a springer spaniel or golden retriever) or very small (for instance, a chihuahua or Yorkshire terrier). Tell the children to colour in the pictures, then cut out each individual picture. The children should then stick their pictures on to their own sheet of paper in the right order—biggest first, right down to the smallest last. Remind the children that, although there was a great difference in size between David and Goliath, God was with David and helped him overcome the giant.

## David versus Goliath Dice

**RESOURCES:** photocopiable sheet (Dice) copied on to thin card; pencils; glue or sticky tape; felt-tips; crayons; graph paper; rulers; scissors; paper and a clipboard to record results

Give each child a copy of the photocopiable sheet (Dice). Explain to the children that they are going to make a dice which shows both Goliath's weapons and armour and David's stone. Remind the children of the story and how David killed Goliath, even though he had only a stone and a sling against Goliath's size, armour and weapons. Tell the children to colour in the pictures on the dice net and write the name of the owner beside each weapon or piece of armour. Next they should cut out the net and make up the dice. When the dice are complete, divide your group into pairs. Tell the children that you want them to roll the dice a hundred times and keep a table of results, they should record which face is uppermost when the dice stops rolling. Show the

children how to make a simple table in which they can enter their results. Remember that Goliath has five faces on the dice, David has only one. When all the dice have been rolled a hundred times, tell the children to convert the results on their table into a simple graph. They should then be able, using their results, to answer the question, 'Is your dice a fair dice?' Discuss how David was able to win against great odds because he was the servant of God.

## Target Game

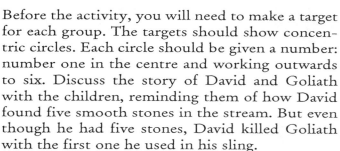

**RESOURCES:** a target for each group; soft foam balls; clipboard and paper to record results; paper; pencils

Before the activity, you will need to make a target for each group. The targets should show concentric circles. Each circle should be given a number: number one in the centre and working outwards to six. Discuss the story of David and Goliath with the children, reminding them of how David found five smooth stones in the stream. But even though he had five stones, David killed Goliath with the first one he used in his sling.

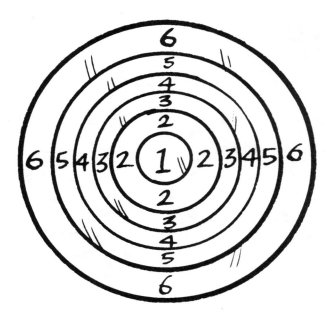

Take your group to a large open area where there is space to play the game in safety. Be sure that the children understand the safety rules involved when they are throwing the balls at the target. Divide the children into evenly sized groups. Tell them that you want them each to have one turn at throwing a soft foam ball at the target. The team should work together to record each person's score. When the throwing activity is complete, sit the children down and discuss what they have done. Tell the children to draw a probability line and ask them to put a cross on it to show the probability of the ball hitting number one.

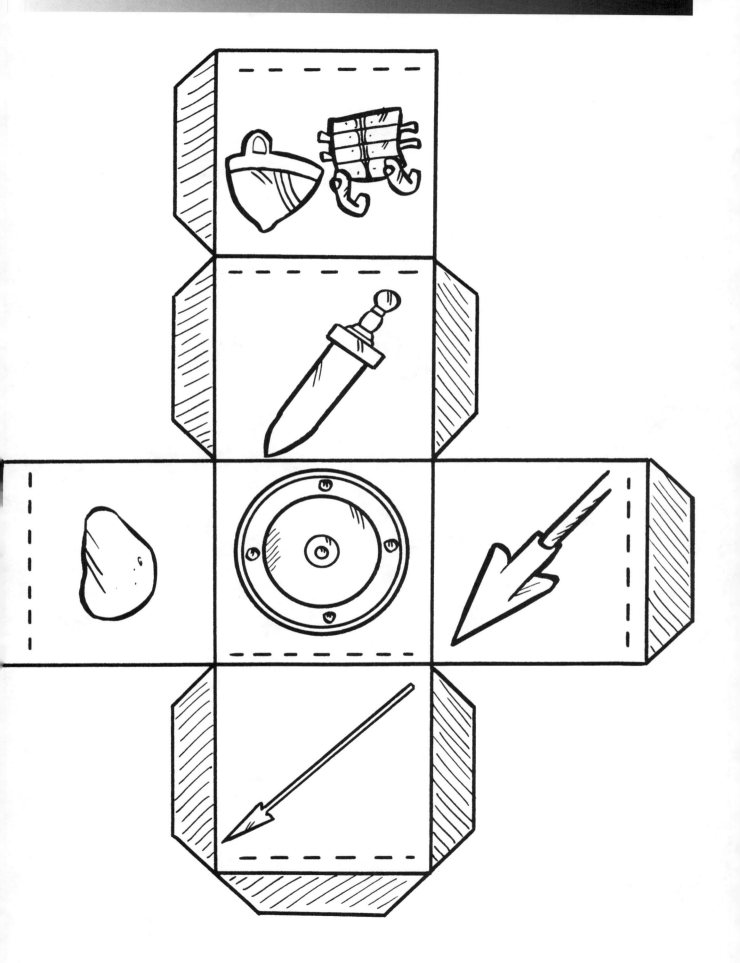

# The Covenant Box

## Exodus 25:10–22

'Make a box out of acacia wood, 110 centimetres long, 66 centimetres wide, and 66 centimetres high. Cover it with pure gold inside and outside and put a gold border all round it. Make four carrying-rings of gold for it and attach them to its four legs, with two rings on each side. Make carrying-poles of acacia wood and cover them with gold and put them through the rings on each side of the box. The poles are to be left in the rings and must not be taken out. Then put in the box the two stone tablets that I will give you, on which the commandments are written.

'Make a lid of pure gold, 110 centimetres long and 66 centimetres wide. Make two winged creatures of hammered gold, one for each end of the lid. Make them so that they form one piece with the lid. The winged creatures are to face each other across the lid and their outspread wings are to cover it. Put the two stone tablets inside the box and put the lid on top of it. I will meet you there, and from above the lid between the two winged creatures I will give you all my laws for the people of Israel.'

### AIM:
## To introduce the Ten Commandments

## NATIONAL CURRICULUM POINTER: SHAPE, SPACE AND MEASURES

## INTRODUCTION

**RESOURCES:** a variety of special boxes with appropriate contents, such as a jewellery box, a biscuit box, a writing box, a sweet box, a hat box, etc.

Show the children the boxes one by one. Ask if the children can guess what each one might contain. Show them what is inside each box. Did they guess correctly? Discuss how boxes can be important. They can be used to keep things safe. Discuss bank deposit boxes and jewellery boxes. Talk about how the contents of the box might affect the box's shape. Tell the children that, in the Bible, God told the Israelites exactly how to make a very special box.

## STORY

**RESOURCES:** photocopiable sheet (Silhouettes); OHP

***Before the assembly, you will need to copy the photocopiable sheet (Silhouettes) and cut out the silhouettes. You should add the relevant silhouette as that part of the box is mentioned.***

Long ago, God gave the people of Israel ten laws he wanted them to keep. The laws were so important that God told Moses, the leader of the Israelites, exactly how to make a beautiful box to keep the laws in. God gave Moses the laws carved on to two slabs of stone. ***(Place the two slabs of stone silhouette on the OHP.)***

God said that the box must be made out of a particular kind of wood which was very long-lasting. The wood was called acacia. God told Moses the exact measurements of the box. He also told Moses to cover the box with pure gold, both inside and out. ***(Place the box silhouette on the OHP and slip the silhouette of the two stone slabs on top of it as if placing them inside.)***

The Israelites did not live in one particular place; they moved around the country, living in tents. So God told Moses that the box must be made easy to carry. He described exactly how he wanted this done. Moses had to make sure that each corner of the box had a gold ring attached to it, so that the carrying-poles would be held in place. ***(Place the carrying-rings and pole silhouettes on the box silhouette.)***

God said that the poles should be made out of the same wood as the box. The poles should also be covered in gold. Once the box had been described to Moses, he was told to make a lid for the box. The lid had to be made only of gold. ***(Place the silhouette of the lid on top of the box.)***

To decorate the lid, Moses was to see that two angel-like figures were made. One would be put on each end of the lid of the box. The figures had to be very carefully made so that they were part of the lid. The angel-like figures, Moses was told, had to face each other over the length of the box, and the wings of the figures must cover the box. *(Place the silhouettes of the angels on the top of the lid of the box.)*

Tell the children how important God's laws are and how we should try our best to keep them ourselves. At this point you may like to show the children a list of the Ten Commandments (see passage below).

# Exodus 20:1–17 (CEV)

God said to the people of Israel:

I am the Lord your God, the one who brought you out of Egypt where you were slaves.

Do not worship any god except me.

Do not make idols that look like anything in the sky or on earth or in the ocean under the earth. Don't bow down and worship idols. I am the Lord your God, and I demand all your love. If you reject me, I will punish your families for three or four generations. But if you love me and obey my laws, I will be kind to your families for thousands of generations.

Do not misuse my name. I am the Lord your God, and I will punish anyone who misuses my name.

Remember that the Sabbath Day belongs to me. You have six days when you can do your work, but the seventh day of each week belongs to me, your God. No one is to work on that day—not you, your children, your slaves, your animals, or the foreigners who live in your towns. In six days I made the sky, the earth, the oceans, and everything in them, but on the seventh day I rested. That's why I made the Sabbath a special day that belongs to me.

Respect your father and your mother, and you will live a long time in the land I am giving you.

Do not murder.

Be faithful in marriage.

Do not steal.

Do not tell lies about others.

Do not want anything that belongs to someone else. Don't want anyone's house, wife or husband, slaves, oxen, donkeys or anything else.

## PRAYERS

Discuss rules and laws with the children. Explain that most rules and laws are made for our own good and we should do our best to keep them. You might choose to use this opportunity to highlight the rules of your group or school. Tell the children that it is sometimes hard to do the right thing but if we ask God he will help us to keep his laws.

---

**Dear God**
**Please help us to keep the rules of our school (or group).**
**You know how hard we find it sometimes.**
**Help us to realize that the rules are there to guide us.**
**Sometimes they keep us safe,**
  **other times they help us to grow into sensible, responsible people.**
**Thank you for the people who care enough about us**
  **to make the rules.**
**Help us to keep them. Amen**

---

**RESOURCES:** a list of the Ten Commandments (It may be more appropriate to use a modern translation of the Bible such as the Contemporary English Version. This passage is quoted above.

Tell the children to sit still and be very quiet while you read the ten laws that God gave us. Ask them to listen carefully. After a moment's silence close the time by saying, 'Thank you God, for the laws which you have given us. Amen.'

Follow up this assembly, enabling the children to practise mathematical skills by using the most appropriate activities for your group from the selection suggested.

# ACTIVITIES

## Group Rules

**RESOURCES:** paper; pencils; crayons; felt-tips; card; glue or sticky tape; tape-measure or ruler; scissors

Discuss rules with the children. You might like to show them a copy of the Ten Commandments. Discuss any rules that the children may know about, such as road safety rules (the Green Cross Code) or rules that you follow in the countryside (the Country Code). Talk about what helps your school or group to run easily even though there are a lot of people involved. Tell the children to try to make up ten rules which they think would be appropriate for their school or group. When the rules have been made up, discuss them with the children and come to a consensus as to which ten are most important. The children could then write out these ten rules and decorate them. You might like to make a box or frame to keep your rules in. You could go on to make a poster-sized copy yourself, which could then be displayed.

## Find a Box Game

**RESOURCES:** photocopiable sheet (Silhouettes)

Before this activity, you will need to decide whether your group will play the game indivi-dually or in teams. If you opt to play the game individually, you will need to copy the photocopiable sheet (Silhouettes) enough times for each child to have one. If you decide to play in teams, you will need to photo-copy the sheet once for each team. After photo-copying, cut out the silhouettes from the sheets and hide them around the playing area. Be sure that your playing area is large enough to play the game safely. When you are ready to play the game, remind the children about the box that God told Moses to have made, in which to keep the stone tablets with the laws on them. Tell the children that hidden around the playing area are enough parts for each person (or team) to make a silhouette of the box described in the story. Show them a completed silhouette, stressing that they must find the 'two tablets of the laws' silhouette, as well as the separate parts of the box. The win-ner is the first child or team to find all the parts needed and complete their silhouette. Discuss with the children how important the laws were which the box contained, and how today we too can try our best to keep those laws.

## Measuring Sheet

**RESOURCES:** photocopiable sheet (Measuring); pencils; felt-tips; crayons; rulers; tape-measures; chalk or coloured sticky tape; scissors

Give each child a copy of the photocopiable sheet (Measuring). Discuss the picture and remind the children about the story and the importance of the box and God's laws which were kept in it. Tell the children that the person in the picture is Moses. Read through the instructions together with the children, then tell them to measure the pictures and fill in the mea-surements on the sheet. When the measurements are complete, the children should colour in the picture carefully. You might like to go on and explain to the children how big the actual box really was. The children could measure out the dimensions of it in a large, suitable space and draw in the outline of the box with chalk, or mark it using coloured sticky tape.

## Make a Box to Fit

**RESOURCES:** a mini-sized chocolate bar for each child; wrapping paper (preferably gold or silver); paper; thin card; scissors; glue; sticky tape; a variety of collage items with which to decorate the boxes; rulers; tape-measure; pencils; a variety of small cardboard boxes with differing 3D shapes

Before this activity, wrap each pre-wrapped mini-sized chocolate bar in gold or silver wrap-ping paper. Discuss boxes with the children; show them the boxes you have collected, point-ing out the 3D shapes involved. Discuss how boxes are made and open out one or two of the examples you have brought, to show the children how they are constructed. Give each child a chocolate bar, telling them to imagine that it is something precious, which they wish to keep safe. Ask the children to make a box to keep their 'precious' item in. Point out the different 3D shapes they might use, such as a cuboid, a cylin-der etc. When the children have worked out and cut out the net of their particular box, they might like to decorate it. They could use collage items such as pasta, coloured paper, lace etc. Next, the children should stick their box net securely together. Finally they should place their 'precious' object in the box, to make sure it fits. Discuss with the children how God told Moses to make a box to keep the laws safe. Remind the children how, if we love God, we should want to

41

keep his laws. At this point you might like to explain what the 'precious' object is and suggest they take it home.

## Covenant Box Collage

**RESOURCES:** a variety of collage materials such as wood-grained paper, foil paper, etc; glue; scissors; calculators (optional); pencils; felt-tips; paper; a Bible for reference

Remind the children of the story about the covenant box. Discuss how Moses knew exactly what God wanted him to do because of the instructions that he was given. Tell the children that you want them to think about the instructions, then make a collage which will show what the covenant box might have looked like. Point out the variety of materials you have provided and encourage them to use them creatively. When the collages are complete, ask the children to write underneath them:

'God told Moses to make the covenant box _____ centimetres long, _____ centimetres wide and _____ centimetres high.
In imperial units of measure this would be _____ inches long, _____ inches wide and _____ inches high.'

You could then convert these collages into a wall display.

## A Row of Angels

**RESOURCES:** paper; paint; brushes; water; protective covering for the floor (if required); tape-measure or rulers; glue; white crêpe paper; coloured paper; scissors

Divide the children into groups, and explain that you want each group to paint a row of angels. The most important thing you want them to do is to make four angels, each of a certain height. Explain that the height of each angel is measured, not from the tip of her wings, but from the top of her head to the bottom of her feet. Tell the children that one angel should measure a metre, the next three quarters of a metre, the next half a metre and the last a quarter of a metre tall. Discuss the options that the children have when it comes to making their angels. They could just paint the angel straight on to the paper. They could draw the angels first, then paint in the features, etc, and then cut them out before sticking them on to coloured paper. They could paint the angels and then go on to collage the wings with white crêpe paper.

When the angels are complete, display them on the walls. Put beside each angel a metre rule and an imperial rule. Encourage the children to compare the two units of measurement. Discuss with the children the covenant box and the angels that God described to Moses. Tell them that God said he would meet Moses at the covenant box and talk with him about the laws.

The following activity is a much longer project than any of the others. The children would very much enjoy taking part in creating their own version of the covenant box, but be aware that it may take several weeks to achieve a finished result and also a considerable amount of advance preparation.

## Make a Full-Sized Model

**RESOURCES:** two or three large cardboard boxes; the materials to make papier-mâché; gold spray-paint; chicken-wire; broom handles; wooden or brass curtain rings big enough for the broom handles to fit through; glue; sticky tape; scissors; gold foil paper; Bibles for reference; string; a copy of the Ten Commandments

The idea is to make a full-sized model of the covenant box. You will need to organize the activity carefully and be very clear about safety rules. Before you start, it would be a good idea to make sure that you and the children have a very clear idea of the dimensions and details of the box. You may like to re-read the story from the Bible (Exodus 25:10–22). To begin with, you need to find a box that will be the basis of the project. You can either find a cardboard box of the right size or make a box of the right size, using the cardboard boxes you have collected. The box needs to be covered with gold foil paper—you could let the children cover the box with glue and apply the paper. Alternatively, you yourself could use gold spray-paint before the activity and bring along a prepared box that has dried. The carrying-rings are made from the curtain rings. If you can find brass it would be more effective; alternatively, cover the wooden rings in a similar way to the box. You will need to make sure that the rings are securely fixed to the box, one ring on each of the bottom corners. One way of doing this is by lacing the ring to the box with string. The broom handles will also need to be covered in either gold foil or gold paint, before they are slotted through the rings.

You will need a very strong piece of card for the lid. Let the children measure it and make a lid which fits exactly. Once made, it should be treated with gold paint or foil in the same way as the box. The 'angels' that sit on the lid should be moulded from chicken-wire, which is then covered with papier-mâché. This particular part of the project will need very careful supervision. Once the 'angels' are dry, they could be covered with glue and torn-up pieces of gold foil. Alternatively, you could use gold paint or gold material. Fix the angels firmly on to the lid using plenty of strong glue. Before putting the completed lid on the box, place a copy of the Ten Commandments inside. Now the box is complete, discuss with the children the importance of what was kept in it.

The covenant box in this picture is _____ centimetres high.

The covenant box in this picture is _____ centimetres wide.

The covenant box in this picture is _____ centimetres long.

The carrying-pole in this picture is _____ centimetres long.

Moses in this picture is _____ centimetres tall from head to toe.

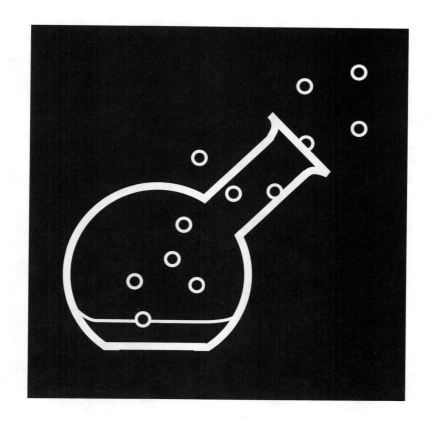

Science

# The Sower

## Mark 4:3–8

'Listen! Once there was a man who went out to sow corn. As he scattered the seed in the field, some of it fell along the path, and the birds came and ate it up. Some of it fell on rocky ground, where there was little soil. The seeds soon sprouted, because the soil wasn't deep. Then, when the sun came up, it burnt the young plants; and because the roots had not grown deep enough, the plants soon dried up. Some of the seed fell among thorn bushes, which grew up and choked the plants, and they didn't produce any corn. But some seeds fell in good soil, and the plants sprouted, grew, and produced corn: some had thirty grains, others sixty, and others a hundred.'

## Mark 4:13–20

Then Jesus asked them, 'Don't you understand this parable? How, then, will you ever understand any parable? The sower sows God's message. Some people are like the seeds that fall along the path; as soon as they hear the message, Satan comes and takes it away. Other people are like the seeds that fall on rocky ground. As soon as they hear the message, they receive it gladly. But it does not sink deep into them, and they don't last long. So when trouble or persecution comes because of the message, they give up at once. Other people are like the seeds sown among the thorn bushes. These are the ones who hear the message, but the worries about this life, the love for riches, and all other kinds of desires crowd in and choke the message, and they don't bear fruit. But other people are like the seeds sown in good soil. They hear the message, accept it, and bear fruit: some thirty, some sixty, and some a hundred.'

## AIM: To demonstrate that listening to God and doing what he says are essential elements of Christian life

## NATIONAL CURRICULUM POINTER: GREEN PLANTS AS ORGANISMS

## INTRODUCTION

**RESOURCES:**

easy-to-grow seeds; compost; plant pot; watering can and water; trowel; light and warmth symbol, e.g. cut-out sun; tray; cloth

Tell the children about planting and growing seeds. Put the tray on a table in front of you where everyone can see it. Gradually introduce the essentials for growing seeds; place each item on the tray as you discuss it. Cover the tray with the cloth, then ask the children who can remember what is on the tray. Choose a representative from each year group to mention one thing that was on the tray. When all the items have been remembered, take the cloth off and go on to plant the seeds. It would be a good idea (after the assembly) to leave the pot of seeds in a place where most of the children can watch their development.

## STORY

*Explain that in the Bible there is a story about sowing seeds, and that the children are going to play a game based on the story. After the game you are going to talk about what the story means, so warn the children to listen carefully and see if they can think of some suggestions.*

*Playing instructions: Before you tell the story, give each class or year group a trigger word. When the trigger word is used in the story, the children are 'triggered' into action. The action is to stand up, turn round and sit down again. Alternatively, if playing with fewer children, divide the children into teams, give each child a trigger word and tell them to run around their team when their trigger word is mentioned. Tell the story of the sower as given below. The words 'sun', 'birds', 'field', 'path', 'gate', 'seed(s)', 'sky' and 'farmer' (in bold) are the trigger words. There are other words that could be used as triggers if you need more, e.g. 'landed'.*

One morning the **sun** was warm, the **sky** was blue and the **birds** were making patterns in the air. The **farmer** took a large bag of **seed** and set off along the **path** to a faraway **field**. He opened the **gate** and watched as the **birds** took flight. He walked slowly to the far end of the **field**, admiring the blue **sky** above him and enjoying the warmth of the **sun** on his shoulders. The **farmer** turned and, plunging his hand into his **seed** bag, grasped a fistful of the small **seeds**. As he walked down the **field** again, the **birds** circled overhead, whilst he threw handful after handful of **seed** over the **field**. His job done, he closed the **gate** and left, but some of the **seed** had landed on the **path**. It was quickly spotted by the **birds**, who flew down from the **sky** to eat it up, the moment the **farmer** had gone. Handfuls of the **seed** had landed on parts of the **field** where the ground was covered with stones. This **seed** soon sprouted over the following days, but on the first hot summer's day the heat of the **sun** scorched the new growth because the roots had not grown deep enough into the soil to be protected. Other handfuls had landed amongst the thorn bushes around the edge of the **field**. These **seeds** sprouted and grew into little plants, but the thorn bushes had been there longer and they took all the goodness from the soil. Although the little plants struggled, they were choked by the prickly bushes. Most of the **seed** had landed on good soil and, after many months of warmth and showers, the **farmer** walked back along the **path** to his **field**. He leant on the **gate** and looked. He had a good crop of corn!

*At the end of the game, ask the children for suggestions about what the story means. Tell them that some of the friends of Jesus asked him to explain the story. Jesus told his friends that he was using the story to show how people hear God's message. The path that the seed landed on is like people who don't really listen to what you tell them: it goes in one ear and out the other! The stones that the seed landed on are like people who think that following God is a good idea, until things get difficult. Then they quickly give up and forget God. The thorn bushes that the seed landed among are like people who follow God but then forget him because they would rather have something else, like lots of money, instead. But some people hear God's*
message and follow him for the rest of their lives. They are like the good soil that the seed landed on.

## PRAYERS

### A Prayer Plant

**RESOURCES:** a large plant pot/container filled with sand; flower shape from photocopiable sheet (Pop-Up Plant); drinking-straws; sticky tape; pencils/crayons

In advance of the assembly, give each class or year group one flower head. Ask them to discuss what they would like to pray about. They should write it on the flower, then stick the flower on to a drinking-straw 'stem' and bring it to assembly.

At the appropriate point in the assembly, remind the children about their prayer flowers and ask a child from each year group to come up and plant the group's prayer flower in the pre-prepared pot/container. Alternatively, for smaller groups, give each child a flower shape and ask them to draw or write in the centre of it what they would like to pray for. Stress that if a child has a private prayer they could just draw a picture of themselves or write their own name, because God knows them and what is in their heart. Tell the children to attach the flower shape to a drinking-straw 'stem' with sticky tape.

Once all the prayer flowers are planted, pray:

---

**Thank you, God, for listening to our prayers. Amen**

---

### A Reflective Prayer

**RESOURCES:** photocopiable sheet (Reflective Prayer) made into OHP slides

Ask the children to be quiet and still as you focus your collective thoughts towards God. Tell them that as you point to each picture in turn and pray 'Help us, God, to listen to you in... [name of the place in the picture]' the children should, in the few moments of silence that follow, think about how listening to God could help them in that particular place. After each of the pictures has been pointed out, end the last silence by thanking God for his care.

Follow up this assembly, enabling the children to think about green plants as organisms by using the most appropriate activities for your group from the selection suggested.

## ACTIVITIES

### A Pop-Up Plant to make

 **RESOURCES:** photocopiable sheet (Pop-Up Plant); scissors; sticky tape; crayons

Give each child a copy of the photocopiable sheet (Pop-Up Plant). Tell the children to colour in the sheet, emphasizing appropriate colours for the various parts of the plant. Discuss and name the parts of the plant and talk about the things a plant needs in order to grow well. Tell the children to cut out their plants and make slits in the plant pot along the dotted lines. They should then thread the tab through the slits. The plant can be made to grow as you remember the story of the sower.

### A Large-Scale Textured Collage

**RESOURCES:** large sheets of paper; glue; scissors; sticky tape; pencils; crayons; felt-tips; large variety of textured collage materials suitable for each section of the story, e.g. sandpaper or loose sand for the path, egg boxes for the stones, silver foil for the thorns, real seed for the sower to sow.

Tell the children to sketch out a large picture of the sower broadcasting the seed. Make sure each part of the story, e.g. the path, the stony ground, etc., is given an area within the collage. The children will need to collage the picture a section at a time, using appropriate textures. As the collage begins to take shape, review the Bible story. As each section of the collage is completed, discuss the growing conditions that the seeds encountered and how and why the conditions affected their germination and growth. When the collage is complete, tell the children to write a short passage about each section of the picture, stressing the germination and growth of the seeds in that particular place. The writing and the collage could then become one large wall display.

### Food

**RESOURCES:** appropriate varieties of bread for the children to try; samples or pictures of different varieties of cereal crop

As the children sample the breads, talk about the story of the sower and how the seed that landed in the good soil produced a large crop. Discuss what crops we use to make bread. Point out the parts of the plant that are used to make bread. Discuss what happens if a grain crop fails to germinate and what a problem this can be for the farmer. Is there a local farmer who would be willing to talk to the children about how he tries to ensure that his crops germinate? Why do the children think a grain crop may fail to germinate?

### Music

**RESOURCES:** a variety of seeds; clean, used plastic containers with lids; materials to decorate the containers; compost

Tell the children to decorate the containers and then experiment to see what kind of sounds the different seeds make when they are sealed into the containers to make a shaker. For instance, a few broad bean or runner bean seeds will sound completely different from an entire packet of cress seeds. Make a range of shakers and tell the children to use them to make up a sound picture of the sower's story. Afterwards select a range of the seeds to plant. When they have germinated, study their growth and compare the plants that are produced. Do they all have the same shaped leaves, etc?

### Looking at Plant Growth

**RESOURCES:** a variety of seeds; compost and plastic plant pots, if required

For younger children (Key Stage One), simply plant some seeds and watch as they grow. Why not try easy vegetables such as radishes or lettuce, as well as flowers?

For older children (Key Stage Two), experiment to discover in what conditions plants grow best. Try planting the same kinds of seeds in different places, like the sower did, and see what happens.

in the classroom

in the playground

at home

out in God's world

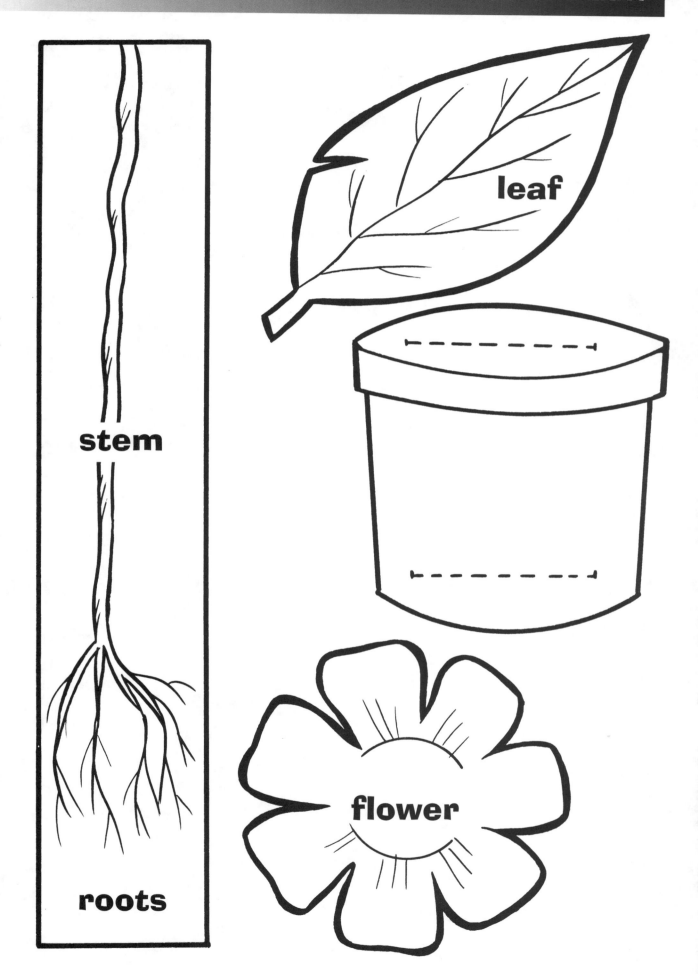

leaf

stem

roots

flower

# One Body with Many Parts

### 1 Corinthians 12:12–27

Christ is like a single body, which has many parts; it is still one body, even though it is made up of different parts. In the same way, all of us, whether Jews or Gentiles, whether slaves or free, have been baptized into the one body by the same Spirit, and we have all been given the one Spirit to drink.

For the body itself is not made up of only one part, but of many parts. If the foot were to say, 'Because I am not a hand, I don't belong to the body,' that would not keep it from being a part of the body. And if the ear were to say, 'Because I am not an eye, I don't belong to the body,' that would not keep it from being a part of the body. If the whole body were just an eye, how could it hear? And if it were only an ear, how could it smell? As it is, however, God put every different part in the body just as he wanted it to be. There would not be a body if it were all only one part! As it is, there are many parts but one body.

So then, the eye cannot say to the hand, 'I don't need you!' Nor can the head say to the feet, 'Well, I don't need you!' On the contrary, we cannot do without the parts of the body that seem to be weaker; and those parts that we think aren't worth very much are the ones which we treat with greater care; while the parts of the body which don't look very nice are treated with special modesty, which the more beautiful parts do not need. God himself has put the body together in such a way as to give greater honour to those parts that need it. And so there is no division in the body, but all its different parts have the same concern for one another. If one part of the body suffers, all the other parts suffer with it; if one part is praised, all the other parts share its happiness.

All of you are Christ's body, and each one is a part of it.

## NATIONAL CURRICULUM POINTER: LIFE PROCESSES AND LIVING THINGS (HUMANS AS ORGANISMS)

**Aim: To show that Christians are all part of one family**

## INTRODUCTION

**RESOURCES:** posters of well-known sports personalities; posters of the teams (football, rugby, hockey) they play in

Display the posters and ask the children how we know which teams the people play for. Discuss the different strips the different teams wear. Point out that the strip identifies the person as a member of the particular team. If the school wears uniform, point out that this too identifies the children as belonging to a particular school.

## STORY

**RESOURCES:** photocopiable sheet (One Body with Many Parts) used as an OHP slide; OHP pens

*Show the OHP slide and discuss the person shown on it. Ask for volunteers from the younger age groups (Key Stage One) to name the parts of the body as you point to them, e.g. foot, arm, hand, head, eye, ear, nose. As the children name them, write the word in the appropriate place. Tell the children that the Bible contains not only stories but also letters. One of the most famous letters is from a man called Paul. He wrote a letter to the people of a city called Corinth. He used the picture of a person to teach them a lesson. Refer to the OHP again and ask, 'If it is a cold day, what is wrong with this picture?' The children should see that the figure has no shoes, hat, scarf or gloves. Go on to ask 'What does it feel like if you have no shoes on? Are just your feet cold or does it feel as if your whole body is cold?' Explain that this shows that your feet are part of your body and the way they feel affects the whole body. Colour in the feet to represent shoes, or draw in the shoes. Repeat the analogy with hat, scarf and gloves.*

Paul told the people of Corinth that each one of them was like a part of the body. Anything that affected one of them affected all of them. This meant that they should look after each other and that no one person was more important than any one else. Christians try to remember what Paul taught them by saying, 'We are all part of the body of Christ.'

## PRAYERS

### A Responsorial Prayer

Explain that you are going to lead the children in a responsorial prayer. First teach the response, asking the children to repeat it after you several times, before trying it on their own. Explain that you will say a sentence of prayer and they will answer with the response.

The response is, 'Help us to look after each other.'

---

**Dear God,
'Help us to look after each other.'
When someone falls over in the playground,
'Help us to look after each other.'
When someone is feeling sad,
'Help us to look after each other.'
When there is something hard to do,
'Help us to look after each other.'
When we are at school,
'Help us to look after each other.'
When we are at home,
'Help us to look after each other.'
Amen**

---

### A Doing Prayer

**RESOURCES:** Cue cards: clap your hands, stamp your feet, touch your head, shout 'hooray', sit quiet and still

Explain to the children that you are going to say a prayer thanking God for making our bodies. You are going to thank God for a particular part of the body and then you will hold up a card telling them what to do.

---

**Dear God, thank you for our wonderful bodies.
Thank you for our hands.**
(Hold up cue card—'clap your hands')
**Thank you for our feet.**
(Hold up cue card—'stamp your feet')
**Thank you for our brains.**
(Hold up cue card—'touch your head')
**Thank you for our voices.**
(Hold up cue card—'shout "hooray" ')
**Thank you for our ears.**
(Hold up cue card—'sit quiet and still'.)
**Thank you, God, that we are part of your wonderful creation.
Amen**

---

Follow up this assembly, enabling the children to think about humans as organisms by using the most appropriate activities for your group from the selection below.

## ACTIVITIES

### Skeleton Puppet

**RESOURCES:** photocopiable sheet (Skeleton Puppet/Cartoon Body Parts); scissors; string; garden cane; sticky tape; split-pin paper-fasteners

Use the photocopiable sheet (Skeleton Puppet/ Cartoon Body Parts) to enable every child to make a skeleton puppet. They should cut out each section of the skeleton round the dotted lines. The two halves of the arm should be joined at the elbow by using a split-pin paper-fastener through the points marked x. The top of the arms should also be connected to the shoulders with a split-pin paper-fastener at the points marked x. The legs should be jointed at the knee in the same way, by using a split-pin paper-fastener at the points marked x. Then the children should use lengths of string secured with sticky tape to attach the skull to the neck and the ribcage to the pelvis. To complete the puppet, they will need to attach a length of string to the skull and to the two hands. These three lengths of string are then attached to a short length of garden cane.

As the children work, discuss with them the purpose of the human skeleton and explain that just as every bone in the skeleton is important so every member of the Christian family is important.

## Gingerbread People

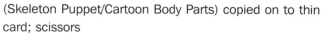

**RESOURCES:** equipment and materials for making gingerbread people, or ready-made but undecorated gingerbread people; glacé icing and dried fruits to decorate

Discuss hygiene and kitchen safety rules with the children and ensure that these are obeyed during the following activity. Together with the children, make gingerbread people. As you cut out and shape the gingerbread people, discuss the main parts of the body represented in the shape: arms, legs, head, etc. When the gingerbread people have been baked and cooled, decor-ate them with the glacé icing. Finish by adding features such as eyes, mouth and nose, by sticking the dried fruit in place with dabs of glacé icing. Discuss families, and suggest that the children take their gingerbread people home to share with their family. Remind the children that Christians are people who are all part of God's family.

## Moving Eye Picture

**RESOURCES:** photocopiable sheet (Moving Eye Picture) copied on to thin card; scissors; crayons

Use the photocopiable sheet (Moving Eye Picture) to enable the children to make a face in which the eyelids move. Tell the children to follow the instructions on the photocopiable sheet, intervening if necessary. When the face is completed, explain that the eye muscles are some of the smallest muscles in the body. They not only allow us to open and close our eyelids but also to move our eyes so that we can read or look at things. You could follow up this activity by going on to discuss how important muscles are to the body and what jobs different muscles do. Discuss the story again and point out that just as different muscles have different jobs, so different members of the Christian family have different jobs but are all of equal importance to the family.

## Music

There are many songs which name parts of the body: for example, 'He gave me eyes so I could see' (Junior Praise), 'Heads, Shoulders, Knees and Toes' or 'The Hokey Cokey'. Choose a selection that the children know and enjoy. Either have a sing-song, listen to the songs on tape or use some percussion instruments to play along.

## Skeleton Hunt

**RESOURCES:** photocopiable sheet (Skeleton Puppet/Cartoon Body Parts) copied on to thin card; scissors

Cut up the skeleton on the photocopiable sheet (Skeleton Puppet/Cartoon Body Parts) into jigsaw pieces. Hide the pieces around your playing area. Challenge the children to find the pieces and put them together to make a skeleton. After the game is over, discuss the skeleton and how it supports the body and helps protect the vulnerable organs. Discuss how Jesus told the Christian family to care for and support one another.

## Different Parts for Different Jobs

**RESOURCES:** paper; pencils; felt-tips; pictures created by disabled artists who use either mouth or foot to control the brush

Tell the children to write their names on a piece of paper. Then tell them to repeat the process using the hand they don't usually write with. Next, suggest that they try to write their names using their toes. Discuss how it feels. Explain that the muscles in their preferred hand have grown used to the fine control needed to write. Show the children the pictures you have brought in and suggest that they attempt to draw a picture with the pencil between their toes. Remind them of the story and how a body, just like the Christian family, is made up of many different parts. Not every part can do every job but there is always a job for every part.

## Name the Part

**RESOURCES:** the body parts from the photocopiable sheet (Skeleton Puppet/Cartoon Body Parts)

Photocopy and cut out the cartoon body parts from the photocopiable sheet (Skeleton Puppet/ Cartoon Body Parts). You will need enough parts for every child to make a body. Tell the children to sit on the floor in a circle and then show the children the cards, discussing the name of each body part as you do so. Then spread the cards across the centre of the circle. Tell the children that you will give them a verbal clue: for instance, 'You wear a watch on this', 'This joins your foot to your leg', 'You wear your T-shirt on this', and so on. The children must then go and look for the body part that they think you mean. Once all the children have found a card, ask them to hold it up. Discuss whether or not it is the correct card and what that body part is called. When all the children have collected a full set of body parts, tell them to stick the cards on to a piece of paper to make a body.

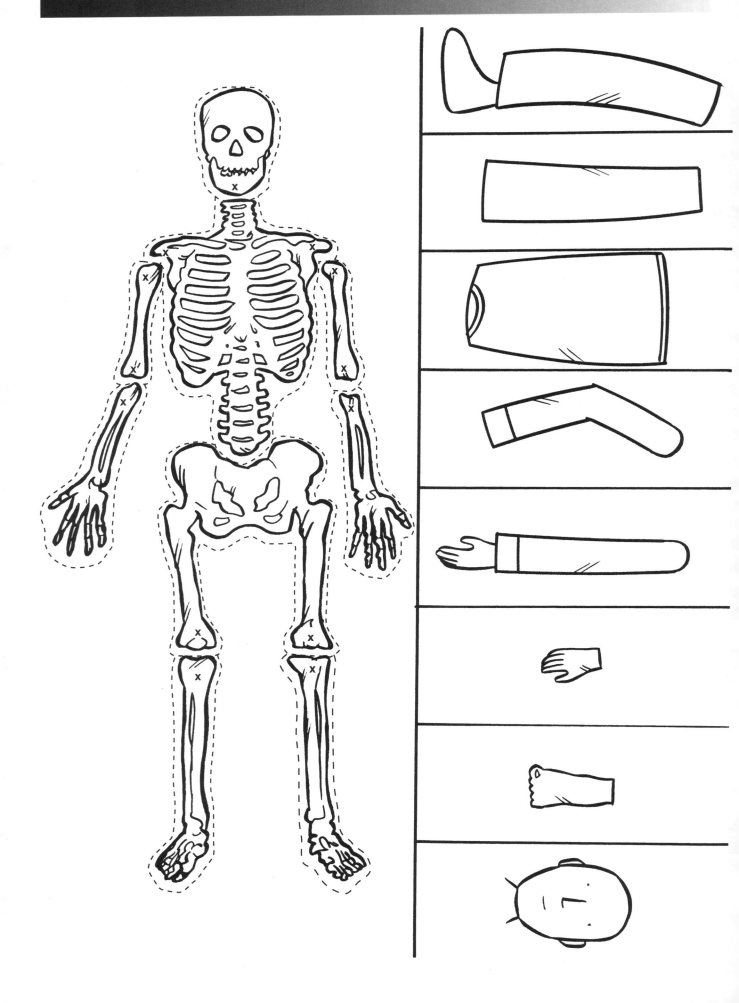

# MOVING EYE PICTURE

1. Cut off bottom third of sheet along the thick black line and keep it safe.

2. Fold remaining paper in half along the dotted line, making sure the face is on top.

3. Cut out the eye sockets from the front half of the folded sheet.

4. Draw the pupil and iris in the eye socket.

5. Colour in face and hair as appropriate.

6. Stick the sides of the folded sheet together to make an envelope.
The opening side should be at the top of the head.

7. On saved piece, cut off the shaded areas.

8. Colour the remaining space on the saved piece the same colour as the face.

9. Put the saved piece of paper into the envelope to cover the pupil and iris.

10. Move the paper up to open the eyes and push it down to close the eyes.

# Jonah and the Whale

### Jonah 1:1–6

One day, the Lord spoke to Jonah son of Amittai. He said, 'Go to Nineveh, that great city, and speak out against it; I am aware how wicked its people are.' Jonah, however, set out in the opposite direction in order to get away from the Lord. He went to Joppa, where he found a ship about to go to Spain. He paid his fare and went aboard with the crew to sail to Spain, where he would be away from the Lord. But the Lord sent a strong wind on the sea, and the storm was so violent that the ship was in danger of breaking up. The sailors were terrified and cried out for help, each one to his own god. Then, in order to lessen the danger, they threw the cargo overboard. Meanwhile, Jonah had gone below and was lying in the ship's hold, sound asleep.

The captain found him there and said to him, 'What are you doing asleep? Get up and pray to your god for help. Maybe he will feel sorry for us and spare our lives.'

### Jonah 1:11–12

The storm was getting worse all the time, so the sailors asked him, 'What should we do to you to stop the storm?' Jonah answered, 'Throw me into the sea, and it will calm down. I know it is my fault that you are caught in this violent storm.'

### Jonah 1:15

Then they picked Jonah up and threw him into the sea, and it calmed down at once.

### Jonah 1:17—2:1

At the Lord's command a large fish swallowed Jonah, and he was inside the fish for three days and nights. From deep inside the fish Jonah prayed to the Lord his God.

### Jonah 2:10—3:3

Then the Lord ordered the fish to spew Jonah up on the beach, and it did. Once again the Lord spoke to Jonah. He said, 'Go to Nineveh, that great city, and proclaim to the people the message I have given you.' So Jonah obeyed the Lord and went to Nineveh.

**AIM: To introduce the idea that God is everywhere**

## NATIONAL CURRICULUM POINTER: PHYSICAL PROCESSES (SOUND)

### INTRODUCTION

**RESOURCES:** a tape of whale songs

Tell the children that sound is a very important part of our world. Without it we would find it difficult to communicate, so it is necessary to  learn to listen well. Ask the children to sit very quietly and listen carefully as you play them a tape. Play the children a few minutes of the tape and then ask them if anybody knows what or who is making the sound. If no one can answer, tell them that it is whales' songs. These songs are the way whales communicate one with another, beneath the sea. The songs allow the whales to talk to each other over a very long distance. Explain to the children that in the Bible there is a story about a large fish—some people think it might have been a whale.

### STORY

**RESOURCES:** script for God, Jonah and Captain; tray and gravel; coins; whale song tape and a tape recorder

*Ask for volunteers to be your sound-effects people: ten children and three adults (or one*

*adult who is vocally versatile). Sit each volunteer by their sound-effect equipment and make sure they understand what they have to do and what the signal will be for them to react to.*

| Character/Sound Effect | Child/Adult | Equipment |
|---|---|---|
| God (speaking part) | adult | script (see words in bold in story below) |
| Footsteps | child | tray and gravel to walk on |
| Payment of fare | child | coins to rattle |
| Storm | children | vocal effects of a storm |
| Sailors | children | shouts for help |
| Captain (speaking part) | adult | script (see words in bold in story below) |
| Jonah (speaking part) | adult | script (see words in bold in story below) |
| Three days in fish | tape | whale song tape and tape recorder |

**Tell the following story, pointing to the character/sound effect at the moment when you wish them to produce the effect.**

One day, God spoke to Jonah. *(Point to the person playing God, who should say,* **'Go to Nineveh and tell the people who live there that I know how wicked they are.'***)*

Jonah didn't want to go, so he went as far away as he could. He thought he could run away from God. He walked to a port called Joppa. *(Point to the person making the footsteps.)*

Jonah found a ship that was sailing to Spain. He paid his fare and went aboard. *(Point to the person who is paying the fare.)*

The ship set sail, but very soon a violent and noisy storm blew up. *(Point to the people who are making the storm effect.)*

The sailors were very frightened. *(Point to the people who are playing the sailors.)*

But Jonah didn't know there was a storm because he was fast asleep in the hold below decks. The Captain went down into the hold and spoke to Jonah. *(Point to the person playing the Captain, who should say,* **'Why are you asleep? Get up and pray for help. We will all be drowned.'***)*

Jonah got up off his bunk and went up on to the deck. The storm got worse and worse. *(Point to the people who are making the storm effect.)*

Jonah knew that the storm was his fault. He had tried to run away from God and ignore what God had told him to do. So Jonah spoke to the sailors. *(Point at the person who is playing Jonah, who should say,* **'Throw me into the sea, if you want the storm to stop.'***)*

Then the sailors threw Jonah into the sea and at once the storm stopped. God sent a huge whale to swallow Jonah. Jonah spent three days in the whale. *(Play a short section of the whale song tape.)*

After three days, God told the whale to spit Jonah out on to the beach. God spoke to Jonah. *(Point to the person who is playing God, who should say,* **'Now will you do what I asked you to do? You cannot run away from me. Go to Nineveh and tell the people I know how wicked they are.'***)*

Jonah now knew that he hadn't been able to run away from God. God had found him, so he listened to God and obeyed him. He went to Nineveh.

**At the end of the story, tell the children to shut their eyes and ask them to listen carefully. Re-run the story without the narration as follows:**

*Point to the person playing God, who should say, 'Go to Nineveh and tell the people who live there that I know how wicked they are.'*

*Point to the person making the footsteps.*

*Point to the person who is paying the fare.*

*Point to the people who are making the storm effect.*

*Point to the people who are playing the sailors.*

*Point to the person playing the Captain, who should say, 'Why are you asleep? Get up and pray for help. We will all be drowned.'*

*Point to the people who are making the storm effect.*

*Point at the person who is playing Jonah, who should say, 'Throw me into the sea, if you want the storm to stop.'*

*Play a short section of the whale song tape.*

*Point to the person who is playing God, who should say, 'Now will you do what I asked you to do? You cannot run away from me. Go to Nineveh and tell the people I know how wicked they are.'*

**At the end, ask the children if they could follow the story by listening to the sounds. Tell the children that God loves us and knows all about us. Even when we think we have managed to run away from him, God will surprise us—he will be there.**

## PRAYERS

### A Noisy Prayer

Tell the children that you are going to say a prayer which thanks God for the loud sounds we all enjoy. At the end of the prayer they should all shout as loudly as they can, 'Thank you, God.'

---

**Dear God,
For brass band music that makes
     us want to march along.
For discos and pop music that
     make us want to dance.
For thunder that rumbles
     through the sky.
For the sound of fast engines in
     aeroplanes and cars.
For the roar of a waterfall and the
     crashing of waves on the shore.
For all the loud noises our ears
     hear in your world.
(Children shout)
THANK YOU, GOD. Amen**

---

### A Quiet Prayer

Tell the children you are going to say a prayer. After each sentence of prayer, you will stop and the children must whisper, 'Help us to listen to your voice.'

---

**Dear God,
When we are worried and don't
     know what to do,
'Help us to listen to your voice.'
When we are frightened and
     scared,
'Help us to listen to your voice.'
When we are angry and want to
     fight back,
'Help us to listen to your voice.'
When we are busy and haven't time
     to stop,
'Help us to listen to your voice.'
In a busy, noisy world,
'Help us to listen to your voice.'
Amen**

---

Follow up this assembly, enabling the children to think about sound by using the most appropriate activities for your group from the selection below.

## ACTIVITIES

## Sound Pictures

**RESOURCES:** photocopiable sheet (Sound Pictures); pencils; crayons; comic books and/or cartoon video

Talk to the children about comic books and cartoons, where sounds are shown in words as part of a picture. Discuss the examples that you have brought in. Give each child a copy of the photocopiable sheet (Sound Pictures). Explain that this sheet shows part of the story of Jonah, with spaces for them to write in the 'sound words' they think are missing. Tell the children to think about the story of Jonah and think what sounds reached the ears of the characters. Remind the children that one of the things Jonah heard was God telling him to go to Nineveh. When the children have drawn their 'sound words', suggest that they colour in the sheets, remembering the story as they do so.

## Sound Diary

**RESOURCES:** A4 paper; stapler; catalogues/magazines; glue; scissors; pencils; crayons

Explain to the children that over the next week they are going to make a sound diary. Give each child several sheets of A4 paper which they can fold in half to make an A5-sized booklet. Make sure that each child's booklet contains one page for every day of the week. Discuss different sources of sound with the children. Tell them to cut out from the magazines and catalogues pictures of different sources of sound, and use them to decorate the cover of their booklet. Tell the children that every day during the following week they should spend ten minutes listening to sounds. Discuss how best they might do this, perhaps by sitting quietly in a garden or a corner of the playground. Tell the children that they should write or draw a picture of all the sounds they hear in their daily listening time, on the appropriate page in their sound diary. Tell the children that many Christians spend some time every day listening and talking to God.

## Music Time

**RESOURCES:** a guitarist or player of a stringed instrument; cardboard boxes (good-quality shoeboxes are ideal); elastic bands of

various sizes; patterned/coloured sticky-back plastic; scissors

Play a tune that the children will recognize on the stringed instrument. Ask them if they can see how the sound is made. Eventually you and the children should be led towards a discussion about the strings and the way they vibrate. You may go on to discuss how the sound is affected by the player pressing on the string in a certain place to produce a particular note. Suggest that the children now make their own 'stringed instrument'. Give each child a cardboard box. Provide them with scissors and patterned or coloured sticky-back plastic to decorate their boxes. Make sure that they do not cover the entire box with the plastic but that they think carefully about their design. Suggest that they cut out shapes or strips to make patterns on their box.

When the decorating of the box is complete, tell the children to stretch a number of elastic bands across the open face of the box. Let the children experiment with the sounds that the elastic bands produce. Emphasize that the vibration of the bands produces the sounds that the children hear. At the end of the project the children and the instrumentalist could spend some time playing and singing favourite songs using the instruments the children have made.

## Sound Survey

**RESOURCES:** photocopiable sheet (Sound Survey); pencils; boards to lean on

Discuss with the children how our world is full of sound. Remind them that, just as sound is all around us, so God is all around us too. Take the children outside to a space where they can see and hear traffic. Make sure that the space you choose is a safe one for this activity. Before you venture outside, give the children a set of safety rules which must be obeyed. Group the children into pairs. Give each child a copy of the photocopiable sheet (Sound Survey). Explain that, for five minutes, one half of every pair will put a tick in the correct column when they **see** a vehicle, etc., while the other half of the pair does the same thing when they **hear** a vehicle, etc., because they will have their back to the sound source. After five minutes, reverse the pairs. At the end of the time, go back inside. Tell each pair to sit down together and compare their results. Did the one who could not see guess correctly each time? How quickly could those who could not see guess what sort of vehicle etc. was making the sound? Bring the children back together and discuss sounds—how we hear sounds when they enter our ears and how sounds get louder as the source comes towards us, and fade away as the source gets further away. As an example, you might discuss thunder. Remind the children of the awful storm that made Jonah realize he could not run away from God. You may like to go back outside again and repeat the activity with a new awareness.

## Food

**RESOURCES:** popping-corn; suitable cooking equipment

As this is a food activity, ensure that all concerned follow the kitchen hygiene and safety rules. Show the children how to make popcorn. While the popcorn is being made, discuss the sound it makes as it cooks. If you use microwave popcorn, discuss the way the bag grows as the corn 'pops'. If you use a conventional stove, discuss the way the pan rattles as the corn 'pops' inside it. Before you share the popcorn, remember to thank God for all his goodness.

# SOUND SURVEY

## I saw

| car | truck/lorry | pedestrian adult | pedestrian child | dogs | aeroplane | horses | emergency services | cyclist | other |
|-----|-------------|------------------|------------------|------|-----------|--------|--------------------|---------|-------|
|     |             |                  |                  |      |           |        |                    |         |       |

## I heard

| car | truck/lorry | pedestrian adult | pedestrian child | dogs | aeroplane | horses | emergency services | cyclist | other |
|-----|-------------|------------------|------------------|------|-----------|--------|--------------------|---------|-------|
|     |             |                  |                  |      |           |        |                    |         |       |

# Light Under a Bowl

## Matthew 5:14–16

'You are like light for the whole world. A city built on a hill cannot be hidden. No one lights a lamp and puts it under a bowl; instead he puts it on the lampstand, where it gives light for everyone in the house. In the same way your light must shine before people, so that they will see the good things you do and praise your Father in heaven.'

## NATIONAL CURRICULUM POINTER: PHYSICAL PROCESSES (LIGHT)

**AIM: To introduce the idea that Christians can be recognized by their actions**

### INTRODUCTION

**RESOURCES:** pictures or posters of items that you cannot easily hide, such as a huge building, a large machine, a city at night, a football crowd, etc.; one object that you can easily hide

Show the children the object that you can hide and then walk around the area, pretending to hide the object in various places while actually taking the opportunity to hide it somewhere about your person. Ask the children where the object is. Eventually reveal that you have hidden it up your sleeve or in your pocket etc. Ask the children if they think it is an easily hidden object. Go on to explain that there are some objects which it is not sensible to try to hide. Use the posters or pictures to illustrate this point.

### STORY

**RESOURCES:** a pre-warned colleague; a large torch; a bucket that will fit over the torch

*Before telling the story, you will need to know if it is possible to make the room dark. Are there curtains you could close? Can you turn the lights off? If you can do neither of these things, you will have to ask the children to pretend that it is very dark at the appropriate moment.*

Start by asking the children, 'When is it dark? What is missing that causes it to be dark?' The children should tell you that the thing that is missing is light/sunshine. Ask the children what we do about the dark. The children should tell you about switching on lights. Go on to discuss lights and the different things that give us light, e.g. the sun, the stars, electricity. At this point a colleague (pre-warned) should turn off the lights, leaving the room in darkness. You may need to reassure some of the younger children. If you cannot darken the room, ask the children to imagine that the room is very dark. Tell the children not to panic, it's all right, you've got a torch. Produce your torch (it should be as big as possible) and switch it on. Talk about how much better it is with a light on. Discuss where it would be best to put the torch so that everybody can see: for instance, on the piano or on the floor. Put the torch in the suggested places and ask the children to vote about which is the best place. Place the torch in the chosen position, then place a bucket over it. The light should now be switched back on. Ask the children if they thought that what you did was very sensible. Explain to the children that in the Bible there is a very famous lesson that Jesus taught, in which he says that Christians are like light. They should let everybody see that they are Christians by the good way they live their lives.

### A Thank You Prayer

**Dear God,**
**Thank you for light. Without it we could not see.**
**Thank you for the sun, which gives us light and warmth.**
**Thank you for the moon and stars, which light up the night.**
**Thank you for fire, which, like the sun, creates warmth and light.**
**Thank you for all the lights of nature—**
    **fire-flies, glow-worms and all the wonders of your world.**
**Amen**

## A Thinking Prayer

**RESOURCES:** torch and bucket from story session

Place the torch on top of the bucket and switch it on. Tell the children that, in the following few moments of silence, you want them to look at the torch, think about light and remember the story they heard.

After a few moments of silence, say, 'Help us, Lord, to be like light to show other people how good you are. Amen'

Follow up this assembly, enabling the children to think about light by using the most appropriate activities for your group from the selection below.

## ACTIVITIES

## Light Sources Mobile

**RESOURCES:** photocopiable sheet (Light Sources Mobile), garden cane; tinsel; scissors; sticky tape; crayons; thread

Tell the children to colour in the light sources on their photocopiable sheet (Light Sources Mobile) before cutting them out along the thick black lines. Show them how to cover a short length of garden cane with tinsel by wrapping it round and round the cane. Make sure that both ends of the cane are securely covered. Tell the children to attach a piece of thread to each light source with sticky tape. Finally they should tie the other end of the thread to the tinsel-wrapped cane. As the children work, talk about light sources and remind them of the story they heard in assembly.

## Drawing Shadows

**RESOURCES:** a sunny day; chalk; paper; pencils; crayons or paint; scissors

Take the children out on to a hard surface where they can draw with chalk. It will need to be a bright, sunny day. Tell the children to get into pairs and draw round each other's shadow with chalk, as the shadows form on the hard surface. Explain why shadows form on a sunny day. You could go on to draw the shadows of groups of children or children posing in unusual stances. When you go back inside, tell the children to draw round each other twice. Colour one shape in black to be their shadow and add features and clothes to the other. Tell the children to cut these shapes out, then make a picture on the wall of them and their shadows. Remind the children that they will need to draw the sun too and position it carefully so that the shadow is in the right place. If space is limited, tell the whole group to make only one or two pictures. Explain to the children that a shadow hides the details of a person or thing. The details of a Christian life should be easily spotted and not hidden because they should be apparent in the good things the Christian does.

## Complete the Picture

**RESOURCES:** photocopiable sheet (Mirror Reflections); small mirrors; pencils; paper; crayons

Discuss light and reflections. Use the photocopiable sheet (Mirror Reflections) and the mirror to allow the children to experiment. Can they complete the pictures using a mirror?

As they complete the candle and the cross, remind them of the story and how Jesus said that

Christians should be like a light which shines 'before people, so that they will see the good things you do and praise your Father in heaven.'

## Catch a Shadow

**RESOURCES:** a sunny day; an outdoor space

Take the children outside on a sunny day. Tell them that they are going to play a sort of 'tig'. One person will be 'it' but instead of 'tigging' a person, the one who is 'it' will have to 'tig' a shadow by jumping on it. The people who are being chased must stand still, the moment their shadow is jumped on. The game will continue until everybody is standing still. Choose a child to be 'it'. Tell all the children to stand in a space by themselves and that when you say 'go' the game will start. The game could be played again by choosing another child to be 'it'.

## Creatures of the Day and Night

**RESOURCES:** white paper; pencils; crayons; pictures of nocturnal creatures (such as bat, badger, moth or owls); pictures of diurnal animals (such as cockerel, butterfly etc.)

Give each child a piece of plain, white A4 paper. Tell them to fold it in half, to A5 size. Then show them how to fold the top sheet lengthways back on itself to the fold, then the bottom sheet lengthways back on itself to the fold, to make a zigzag shape. When the sheets are opened out, there will be four lengthways sections.

Discuss with the children the subject of day and night. Point out that some animals prefer to come out at night-time when it is dark. Discuss which animals these might be and why. Show the children the pictures of the nocturnal creatures and tell them to draw one in each section of their page. Now tell the children to turn their sheets of paper over. Be careful how they do this because you must ensure that the creatures drawn are drawn the same way up on both sides of the paper. Discuss diurnal creatures, show the pictures and tell the children to draw one creature in each section. They should label the appropriate sides 'day' and 'night'. You could go on to discuss how easy it is to see creatures of the day but how creatures of the night are difficult to see. In the same way it should be easy to recognize a Christian because you can see the good things they do.

## Sunshine Window

**RESOURCES:** a variety of paper and materials—some opaque, some clear and some translucent, such as silver foil, tissue paper, cellophane, tracing paper, coloured paper or card; thin card; scissors; glue; sticky tape

Tell the children that they are going to make a window which shows a picture of the sun. The window should be made to resemble a stained-glass window, using card or thick black paper where the lead would be and coloured paper of some sort where the glass would be. Divide the children into groups and tell each group to make a window, but ensure that each group uses a different selection of materials for the coloured image. When the windows are complete, use Blu-tack to stick them on to the window panes in your room. Tell the children to study them carefully at different times of the day over a period of time. Bring the project to a close by discussing how light does or does not come through the windows they have made. Which ones does it come through? Why is this so? Discuss stained-glass windows, how they are often seen in churches and how the story that was told in assembly could be interpreted in a stained-glass window.

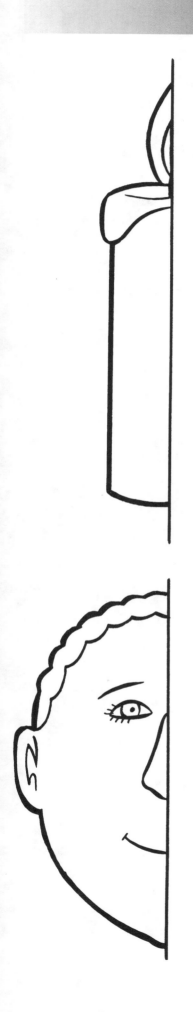

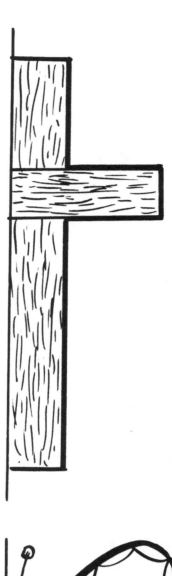

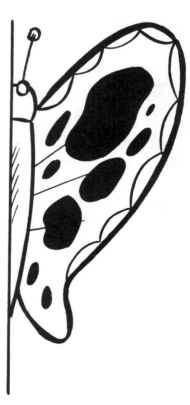

Design and Technology

# The Tower of Babylon

## Genesis 11:1–9

At first, the people of the whole world had only one language and used the same words. As they wandered about in the East, they came to a plain in Babylonia and settled there. They said to one another, 'Come on! Let's make bricks and bake them hard.' So they had bricks to build with and tar to hold them together. They said, 'Now let's build a city with a tower that reaches the sky, so that we can make a name for ourselves and not be scattered all over the earth.'

Then the Lord came down to see the city and the tower which those men had built, and he said, 'Now then, these are all one people and they speak one language; this is just the beginning of what they are going to do. Soon they will be able to do anything they want! Let us go down and mix up their language so that they will not understand one another.' So the Lord scattered them all over the earth, and they stopped building the city. The city was called Babylon, because there the Lord mixed up the language of all the people, and from there he scattered them all over the earth.

**AIM: To emphasize the importance of God in our lives**

**NATIONAL CURRICULUM POINTER: DESIGNING/MAKING SKILLS, KNOWLEDGE AND UNDERSTANDING**

## INTRODUCTION

**RESOURCES:** photocopiable sheet (Towers) used as OHP slides

Use the photocopiable sheet (Towers) as a series of OHP slides to illustrate a discussion about famous towers. Ask if the children have visited any of the towers in the pictures. Discuss why people might build a tower and what it feels like when you are at the top of a very tall tower. Tell the children about a visit you have made to a tower.

## STORY

**RESOURCES:** an adult who can speak a language the children are not familiar with; a selection of empty cardboard boxes

*Tell the children that in the Bible there is a very old story.* The Bible says that, at that time, everyone on earth spoke the same language and lived in the same area. The people wanted to live in a beautiful city with proper houses. But they didn't stop and ask God what they should do. They just went ahead and designed a city with a tower that reached to the sky. They started to make bricks and used tar as mortar. Soon their city was beginning to take shape and they began to build the tower, but still they didn't talk to God about what they were doing. *(Choose two or three children to come and help build a tower from the empty boxes. Tell them that they may not speak to each other, but have to do exactly what they are told. Give them very careful instructions in English, such as, 'Put that very big box as the base... now use that box and make sure that it's right in the centre of the base...')* God came and looked at the building work and was very sad because the people had forgotten all about him. He decided that the people had to learn to trust him.

*(At this point, ask the other adult to take over, giving the building instructions in a language with which the children are not familiar. The children will not be able to complete the tower and it might fall down.)* God made the people speak lots of different languages and they could not understand each other. They couldn't go on building the tower because they couldn't understand each other, just as the children building the tower can't understand what they are being told to do. We should always remember that it is important to trust God and ask him for help with everything we do.

## PRAYERS

Tell the children to be very quiet and still as you focus your collective thoughts towards God. Use one or both of the following prayers.

**Dear God,**
**Help us to remember that we**
**should ask you for help with**
**everything we do.**
**(Mention aloud some of the**
**forthcoming activities that you know**
**the children will be involved in.)**
**Thank you, God, that you are with**
**us all the time. Amen**

**Dear God,**
**We see your power in the wonder**
**of the galaxy:**
**the fiery comets that hurtle**
**through space;**
**the creativity of your hand in the**
**endless pattern of the planets.**
**Yet you have time for us.**
**Time to listen, time to help**
**and time to care, if we will only**
**ask you.**
**Please be very close to us all**
**this day. Amen**

Follow up this assembly, enabling the children to practise designing and making skills by using the appropriate activities for your group from the selection below.

## ACTIVITIES

### A Tower Competition

**RESOURCES:** a collection of materials suitable for making a tower, such as newspaper; construction kits; cardboard boxes etc.

Divide the children into small groups. Tell them you are going to have a competition to see who can build the tallest tower. Give each group a different type of material. Tell the children to design their tower carefully before making it. After a given space of time, measure to see which group has made the tallest tower. Discuss why their tower was the tallest: was it due to the design, the materials, the construction or something else? Ask the children to consider which of the towers is the strongest and which the most attractive. Can they give reasons for their decision? During this activity, remind the children that the people of Babylon wouldn't talk to God about their tower to reach the sky, and how it is important for us to talk to God about our daily lives.

### Design a Tower

**RESOURCES:** appropriate reference books; paper; pencils; crayons; OHP slides used in the introduction to the assembly

Discuss with the children different sorts of towers, using the OHP slides to illustrate the discussion. Explain that towers are built for many different reasons and purposes. For instance, there is a famous tower in Paris that was built to celebrate an exhibition. Towers are used as office blocks, flats and hotels. Some smaller towers were built as a reminder of people or events. Industry uses towers too, for example, to store water. Suggest that the children use the reference books to find out about towers before they go on to design a tower for a specific purpose. Their tower could celebrate a special occasion, or remind people about an event or person. It could be a block of flats. The choice is theirs. When the designs are complete, make them into a display and evaluate them with the children.

### Tower Sandwiches

**RESOURCES:** brown and white bread; a variety of sandwich fillings and spreads; pastry cutters; sandwich-making equipment

Discuss the hygiene and kitchen safety rules with the children and make sure that the rules are obeyed during the following activity. Discuss sandwiches and the different fillings you can use. Discuss tastes that go well together, and healthy food. Tell the children to design a healthy tower sandwich. Point out that they could use a mixture of breads as well as different fillings between each layer. How many sandwiches high would be sensible in a tower sandwich? Does a particular shape of sandwich (square, triangular or circular) make a more stable tower? Evaluate the designs, then tell the children to make their tower sandwiches. Before you sit down to share the sandwiches together, stop and thank God for all his goodness.

# A Weight-Bearing Tower

**RESOURCES:** a collection of materials suitable for making a tower, such as newspaper, construction kits, cardboard boxes, etc.; a weight, such as a book

Divide the children into small groups and tell each group to design a tower, like the one in the story, but their tower must be able to support a book (or the chosen weight). Tell the children they may choose their own materials and method of construction. Once the designs have been completed, the children should go on to build their tower. After all the towers have been tested with the weight, discuss them all and evaluate which method of construction was the most successful. If any towers failed to support the weight, could the children think of ways to reinforce or strengthen their design to make it strong enough to support the weight? It may be appropriate during this activity to tell the children that just as a tower needs to be strengthened to withstand storms and winds, so we need to strengthen our lives with prayer.

# Brick Bonds

**RESOURCES:** photocopiable sheet (Brick Bonds); scissors; glue; crayons; pencils; construction kits

Tell the children to use the construction kits to make a small wall. When the walls are finished, look at them together. Explain that if you want to make a strong wall you have to be sure that you don't put bricks directly one on top of the other. The pattern that the bricks make is called the bond. Use the photocopiable sheet (Brick Bonds) to introduce the children to various brick bonds. Point out the different patterns and explain that when you build a wall you have to be careful that the spaces between the bricks do not make one long straight line up the length of the wall. Different brick bonds are used for different sorts of walls.

**How to make up the 'walls' on the Brick Bonds sheet:** Colour in the walls. Cut along the thick black lines. Fold along the dotted lines. Stick A to A, B to B, C to C and D to D. The walls should then stand up by themselves.

When the children have made up the 'walls' on the Brick Bonds sheet, ask them to use the construction kits again to make a stronger wall. During this project opportunities will arise to remember the story of the tower of Babylon and how the people couldn't finish their tower because they forgot to talk to God.

# ✚ EXTENSION ACTIVITY

Organize a walk for the children, either around the school or around the neighbourhood, to look at the different sorts of brick bonds that are used in local buildings or walls. Take rubbings of interesting bonds you find and use them to make a display.

# TOWERS

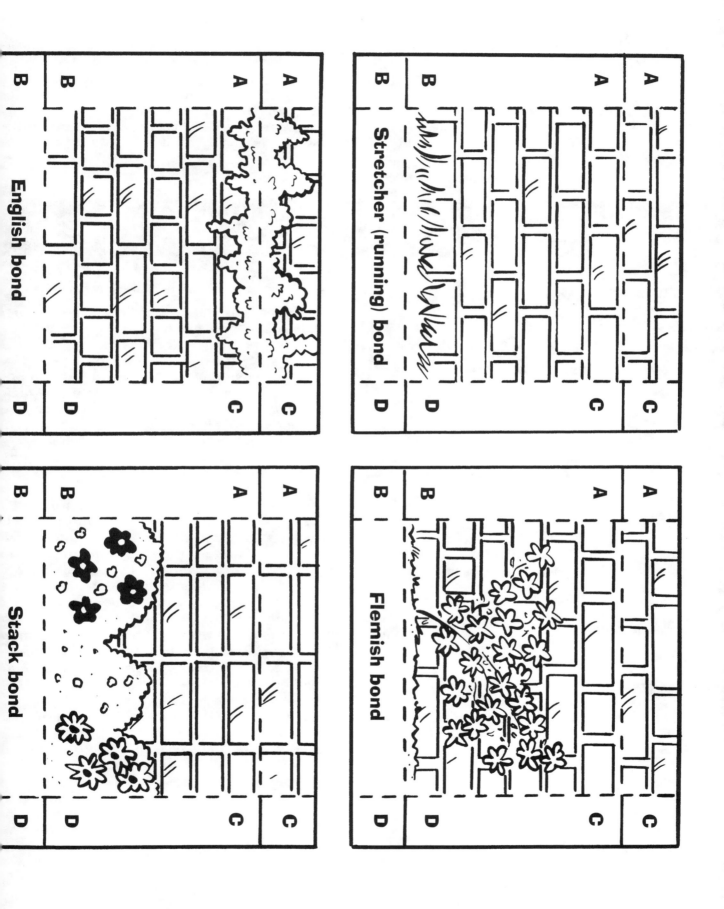

Stretcher (running) bond

English bond

Flemish bond

Stack bond

# Jesus Shares a Meal

## 1 Corinthians 11:23–25

For I received from the Lord the teaching that I passed on to you: that the Lord Jesus, on the night he was betrayed, took a piece of bread, gave thanks to God, broke it, and said, 'This is my body, which is for you. Do this in memory of me.' In the same way, after the supper he took the cup and said, 'This cup is God's new covenant, sealed with my blood. Whenever you drink it, do so in memory of me.'

**AIM: To introduce the idea that Christians remember Jesus when they celebrate the Eucharist**

## INTRODUCTION

**RESOURCES:** pictures of the items needed to lay a table; Blu-tack; paper; pens; large picture of an empty table covered with a cloth

Tell the children that you are going to lay a table for a meal. Ask for suggestions of the things you would need. As each item is mentioned, ask the child who suggested it to come and place it on your large picture of an empty table. Ensure that eventually each item is laid in the correct place. Tell the children about a particular meal you remember, who was there and what you were celebrating. Write a word or two about your meal on a piece of paper and stick it on to the table-cloth. For instance, you could write 'Family Christmas'. Select one or two children to recount their memories and add these to the cloth too. Lead into the story by explaining that in the Bible there is a very special meal which Christians still celebrate today.

## STORY

**RESOURCES:** two P.E. benches or a large low table; one or two cushions; paper plates and cups; jug of blackcurrant

squash; a basket with a loaf of 'home-baked' bread

*Walk over to the P.E. benches and explain that Jesus and his twelve friends shared a special meal. Ask for twelve volunteers to come and sit around the benches. Point out that, in those days, tables were low and people sat on the floor or, if they were very lucky, on cushions. Give one or two of the children a cushion to sit on. Explain that Jesus had sent two of his friends, Peter and John, to get the meal ready, so there would have been some plates (offer paper plates to the children to place on the table), some drinking cups (paper cups), some wine (a jug of blackcurrant squash) and some bread (offer a basket with obviously 'home-baked' bread in it. This bread will be shared amongst all the children so it is a good idea to pre-mark it into sections, one for each group). Hold up the jug and the bread and tell the children that Jesus made the bread and wine special when he blessed it. He told his friends to eat it and remember him every time they broke bread or drank wine. Send the children back to their places and tell everybody that today Christians still use bread and wine that has been blessed as a way of sharing a meal with Jesus and remembering what he said and did. It would be appropriate to point out to the children at this point that the special meal has many names, such as the Eucharist, Holy Communion, the Lord's Supper, the Holy Sacrament.*

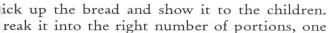

## PRAYERS

### A Meditative Prayer

**ESOURCES:** the basket of 'home-baked' read used in the story; paper plates

ick up the bread and show it to the children. reak it into the right number of portions, one for each year group. Ask for one child from each year group to come and fetch a paper plate with their group's bread. Tell them to take it back to their group and share it out, a small piece for everyone. Ask everybody to sit quietly, holding their bread in the palm of their hand. Tell them to look at it while you say the following prayer.

---

**Thank you, God, for grain; for the way a tiny,**
    **dry seed grows into a sturdy plant.**
**Thank you for sunshine and rain, which help the grain to ripen.**
**Thank you, God, for the farmers,**
    **who work hard to gather in the harvest.**
**Thank you for the factories where the grain is turned into flour.**
**Thank you, God, for the bakers,**
    **who use their skills to make our bread.**
**Thank you for the smell and taste of new-made bread. Amen**

---

fter the prayer, tell the children that they may ow eat their bread.

### Jigsaw Prayer

**ESOURCES:** picture of a celebration meal, cut into saw pieces (you should allow one piece for each group children)

Tell everyone to be quiet and still as you focus your collective thoughts towards God.

Say the following prayer, inviting one child from each group to bring up their section of the jigsaw at various appropriate moments throughout the prayer.

---

**Almighty God,**
**Thank you for food, and the memories we have of celebration meals:**
**Times when we can be together and share with others,**
**Times of happiness and joy with family and friends,**
**Times we can remember with pleasure in later years. Amen**

---

ollow up this assembly, enabling the children to ractise designing and making skills by using the ost appropriate activities for your group from e selection below.

## ACTIVITIES

### A Banner Project

**ESOURCES:** pictures of symbolic presentations of the Lord's Supper or the tual item depicting it, such as a banner or a eeler; sewing materials; glue; felt; paper; various xtures of card; scissors; pencils; felt-tips

Remind the children of the story they heard. Explain that, as it is very important for Christians, many churches make a symbolic representation of the bread and wine, perhaps as a banner, a stained-glass window or a kneeler. Show them some pictures or actual objects that do this. Explain that the children are going to make a banner. Discuss what materials they could use and how it could be made. They could consider sewing material or sticking felt or paper or making the banner with various textures of card. Divide the children into small groups and ask them to draw out their design and come up with some ideas for the materials needed. After discussion, they should go on to make the banner. You could then display the banners and evaluate them.

## A Memory Wheel to Practise Making Skills

**RESOURCES:** one copy of the photocopiable sheet (Memory Wheel) for each child; scissors; split-pin paper-fasteners; felt-tips; crayons; pencils

Give out the photocopiable sheets (Memory Wheel). Talk about memories. Suggest that each child thinks about four happy memories; maybe some children would be willing to talk about their choices. Tell the children to draw a picture of one memory in each section of the circle on the sheet. Ensure they colour in their memory pictures and draw them the right way up (remember that the wheel will rotate). Help them to cut out the circle and make a small hole in the centre. Next, cut the rectangle from the sheet and very carefully cut out the window segment. Make a small hole in the place marked. Decorate the rectangle and colour in the writing. Then help each child position their memory circle in the correct place behind their rectangle. Attach the circle and the rectangle together with a split-pin paper-fastener pushed through the small holes you have made. Show the children how to move the memory wheel so that a memory is displayed in the window. Remind them that Christians remember Jesus at a special meal.

## A Celebration Foods Board Game to Make

**RESOURCES:** for each group of four children, photocopy the Game Board once on to thin card, and cut out the person counters. For each child, photocopy the place-mat sheet (Place-Mat and Menus). Photocopy the food items (from Place-Mat and Menus) just once, and cut into individual squares (there is one set of food for each celebration); scissors; felt-tips or crayons; dice; shaker; sticky-back plastic

Show the children the sheets you have copied and tell them they are going to make a board game to play. Talk about the four celebrations (Easter, Christmas, Birthdays and Harvest) and the special food eaten on these occasions. Talk about preparing for celebrations, discussing with the children their own experiences. Ask them to colour in their person counters and place-mat. To preserve the game, cover each part of it with sticky-back plastic. You could ask the children to design and make a box to keep the game in. Once the children have made the game, tell them to evaluate it and suggest ways in which it could be improved.

How to play the game: There are four players. Each player has a person counter and a place-mat. All the person counters are placed on the empty table to start. The individual food items are placed around the board. Each player collects the four items of food relating to their person counter. In turn, each player must throw a six to start, and can choose which path away from the table they want to take. They must then throw the dice to continue around the track, following the instructions as they land on them. They pick up a food item as they land on the appropriate square and place the item they have collected on their place-mat. If a player lands on a food item relating to someone else's person counter, they should ignore it. When a player has collected all their food they must continue around the board until they are able to find a path and return to the table. The first player to return to the table is the winner.

## Making Bread

**RESOURCES:** packets of bread mix or the ingredients (including live yeast) to make bread

Discuss hygiene and kitchen safety rules with the children and make sure that the rules are obeyed during the following activity. Make bread, experimenting to see what different shapes the dough can be made into, such as plaits, rolls or even mice! For younger children you could use a bread mix which simply needs water adding to it. Older children would enjoy discovering the properties of live yeast and how this affects the rising of the dough.

## ✚ EXTENSION ACTIVITY

If there is a special event coming soon or even if there isn't, why not plan a meal together? It could be as simple as a picnic, or a more formal occasion to which you invite a special guest. Involve the children in as many aspects of the organization as is feasible. This should include designing and making such things as invitations, menus, place-mats and name cards. A ploughman's-style meal is an easy cold option; jacket potatoes served with a variety of fillings would provide a hot, nutritious alternative. Whatever food you choose to prepare, make sure kitchen safety and food hygiene rules are observed.

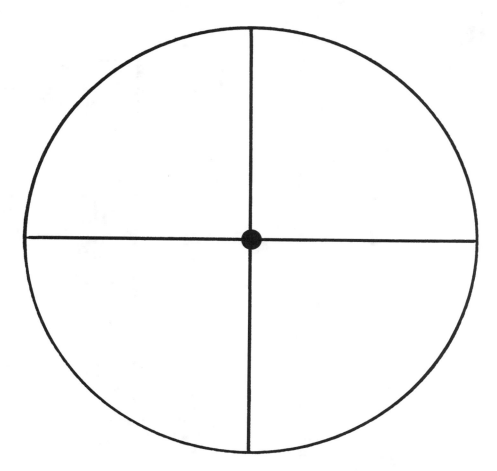

Thank you, God, for happy memories

# GAME BOARD

| Easter Egg | Go Back 1 | | Toffee Apple | | | Miss a Turn | Meringue Snowman | |
|---|---|---|---|---|---|---|---|---|

| | | | Throw a 6 | | | | Go on 2 |
|---|---|---|---|---|---|---|---|

| | Christmas Pudding | | Throw a 6 | | | Throw a 6 | |
|---|---|---|---|---|---|---|---|

**Simnel Cake**

| | | Go on 3 | | Go on 2 | Box of Chocolates | | Go back 4 |
|---|---|---|---|---|---|---|---|

| Roast Lamb | | Sand-wiches | Cottage Pie | | | | |
|---|---|---|---|---|---|---|---|

| Miss a Turn | | | Miss a Turn | | Christmas Cake | Go back 4 | Ice-cream |
|---|---|---|---|---|---|---|---|

| Apple Pie | | | | | | | Go on 3 |
|---|---|---|---|---|---|---|---|

| | Turkey | Go on 4 | | Birthday Cake | | Fruit cake | |
|---|---|---|---|---|---|---|---|

| | | | | | | Go back 2 | Pancakes |
|---|---|---|---|---|---|---|---|

**Treat**

**Cake**

**Main course**

**Pudding**

| | | | |
|---|---|---|---|
| Easter egg | Meringue Snowman | Box of Chocolates | Toffee Apple |
| Simnel Cake | Christmas Cake | Birthday Cake | Fruit Cake |
| Roast Lamb | Turkey | Sandwiches | Cottage Pie |
| Pancakes | Christmas Pudding | Ice Cream | Apple Pie |

# Jesus Changes Simon's Name

### John 1:35–42

The next day John was standing there again with two of his disciples, when he saw Jesus walking by. 'There is the Lamb of God!' he said.

The two disciples heard him say this and went with Jesus. Jesus turned, saw them following him, and asked, 'What are you looking for?'

They answered, 'Where do you live, Rabbi?' (This word means 'Teacher'.)

'Come and see,' he answered. (It was then about four o'clock in the afternoon.) So they went with him and saw where he lived, and spent the rest of that day with him.

One of them was Andrew, Simon Peter's brother. At once he found his brother Simon and told him, 'We have found the Messiah.' (This word means 'Christ'.) Then he took Simon to Jesus.

Jesus looked at him and said, 'Your name is Simon son of John, but you will be called Cephas.' (This is the same as Peter and means 'a rock'.)

### Matthew 16:13–18

Jesus went to the territory near the town of Caesarea Philippi, where he asked his disciples, 'Who do people say the Son of Man is?'

'Some say John the Baptist,' they answered. 'Others say Elijah, while others say Jeremiah or some other prophet.'

'What about you?' he asked them. 'Who do you say I am?'

Simon Peter answered, 'You are the Messiah, the Son of the living God.'

'Good for you, Simon son of John!' answered Jesus. 'For this truth did not come to you from any human being, but it was given to you directly by my Father in heaven. And so I tell you Peter: you are a rock, and on this rock foundation I will build my church, and not even death will ever be able to overcome it.'

---

## NATIONAL CURRICULUM POINTER: DESIGNING/MAKING SKILLS

**AIM: To introduce the idea that people who love us choose our names**

### INTRODUCTION

**RESOURCES:** two large birth celebration banners, one pink, one blue (try greeting-card shops)

Ask some children to come and help you. Divide them into two groups and give each group a banner to unroll and display. As they hold the banners up, ask the rest of the school what they think has happened. When they tell you a baby has been born, ask what they think the baby's name might be. Choose individuals to suggest names and perhaps share how they got their names. Explain that some Christians call a baby's naming ceremony a 'christening'.

### STORY

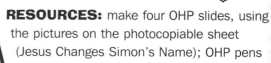

**RESOURCES:** make four OHP slides, using the pictures on the photocopiable sheet (Jesus Changes Simon's Name); OHP pens

*Explain that in the Bible Jesus changed somebody's name because he had a very special job for that person. Show OHP 1 and tell the children that one day Simon's brother, Andrew, came running up to him. Andrew said that he and a friend had found Jesus. Show OHP 2 and tell the children that Andrew took his brother to meet Jesus.* When Jesus saw Simon, he recognized him and said, 'Your name is Simon son of

John, but you will be called Cephas.' Everybody knew that Cephas was the same as Peter. So Jesus had changed Simon's name to Peter. **Explain that every name has a meaning and Peter means 'rock'.** Elsewhere in the Bible Jesus explained why he changed Simon's name to Peter. Jesus knew that he would be returning to his Father in heaven but that Peter would remain on earth to help look after his followers. People who follow Jesus are called Christians and are sometimes called his Church. **Show OHP 3 and ask the children what words they can see in the pattern. As Peter is mentioned, colour in PETER, and ROCK as rock is mentioned. Finish by explaining that Jesus said that Peter would be the rock on which he would build his Church. Place OHP 4 on top of OHP 3 to provide an outline round the word pattern, thus making it clear that the word pattern is a stylized church.**

## PRAYERS

### An Acrostic Prayer

**RESOURCES:** five large signs, each with a capital letter spelling the word NAMES.

Choose five older children to come out and help you. Give each child a letter, making sure that they stand in the order NAMES. Ask them to lift their letter up when you say the name of their letter. Tell everyone to be quiet and still as you focus your collective thoughts towards God.

> **Names are very important.**
> **All are special to you.**
> **Maker God, you know us,**
> **Everyone, through and through.**
> **Send your blessings upon us,**
>    **and bring us closer to you.**
> **Amen**

At the end of the prayer, ask the children if they saw what happened and point out that the first letter of each line began with a letter of the word NAMES. Tell them this is called an acrostic prayer.

### A Responsorial Prayer

Explain that you are going to lead the children in a responsorial prayer. First teach the response, asking the children to repeat it after you several times before trying it on their own. Explain that you will say a sentence of prayer and they will answer with the response.

The response is, 'Thank you, God, that I am special.'

---

> **Dear God,**
> **You have given us all different gifts and talents.**
> **'Thank you, God, that I am special.'**
> **You gave us all unique patterns on our fingertips.**
> **'Thank you, God, that I am special.'**
> **You gave us wonderful brains.**
> **'Thank you, God, that I am special.'**
> **We can make our own decisions.**
> **'Thank you, God, that I am special.'**
> **People who love us chose our names.**
> **'Thank you, God, that I am special.'**
> **Amen**

---

Follow up this assembly, enabling the children to practise designing and making skills by using the most appropriate activities for your group from the selection below.

## ACTIVITIES

### A Working-with-Fabric Project based on Luke 10:20

**RESOURCES:** sewing materials (hessian or binca); felt; brightly coloured threads; large-eyed rounded-point needles; thin card; glue; graph paper; pencils; crayons; scissors

Remind the children of the acrostic prayer; talk about names and how special they are. Provide reference books to enable the children to find out the meaning of their own names. Tell the children that in the Bible it says, 'Be glad because your names are written in heaven.' Explain that they are going to sew their names and a representation of the meaning on to material. Discuss various ways of laying out their design (e.g. either horizontally or vertically), and the sorts of stitches and materials they might use. Give them a piece of graph paper to draw their design on and, after further discussion, encourage them to complete it. When they have finished, turn the edges of the material under and stick the work on to thin card, pointing out that this will stiffen the work, enabling them to turn it into a picture or wall hanging. For younger children, or for speed, as an alternative to sewing, try using felt as a backing and different coloured felt letters which the children can stick on to it. You may need to provide card templates if the children find freehand cutting difficult. The felt can still be mounted on the card to stiffen it.

## A Model of a Christening

**RESOURCES:** pictures and photographs of the main elements of a christening; cardboard boxes; glue; scissors; paint; pencils; paper; a collection of junk modelling materials

Lead a discussion with the children about a Christian naming ceremony for a baby. Have any of them been to one? Show them pictures or photographs of the main elements of a christening, such as the building where it takes place and the people who are present. Ask for suggestions as to how you could make a 3D model of the ceremony. Talk about the different types of materials you could use (such as card, paper, balsa wood, junk, material or papier-mâché) and the various ways you could make models of people. Divide the children into groups and give them some time to design their own model. They might like to draw or use a small collection of 'junk' to work out their design. After further discussion encourage them to choose suitable materials and make their model.

## A Door Hanger to Evaluate

**RESOURCES:** photocopiable sheet (Door Hanger); card; paper; crayons; felt-tips; scissors; sticky-back plastic

Use the photocopiable sheet (Door Hanger) so that each child makes a door hanger by adding colour to it in the way that they prefer, then cutting it out. Find a variety of door knobs to look at and discuss whether the door hangers they have made are the most suitable for the door knob they intend to use it on. Tell the children to design a door hanger which would be suitable for their own door knob. When the door hangers are complete you could discuss how long they will last and what the children could do to make them more durable.

## Design a Table Layout for a Party

**RESOURCES:** collage materials; disposable tableware; dried flowers; paper streamers etc.; glue; crayons; felt-tips; pencils; scissors

Discuss parties which are held to celebrate a baby's naming ceremony. Divide the children into groups and tell them to design a picture of a table layout, showing the food and decorations ready for a party which follows a baby's naming ceremony. When the designs are complete, discuss them with the children. Tell them to continue and make their layout in a 3D form, using the collage materials to create the food and the disposable tableware to represent the crockery and cutlery.

## Music

**RESOURCES:** tape of a lullaby; materials with which to make simple percussion instruments

Play the children a lullaby and discuss what is special about a lullaby. Talk about soft music and sounds. Help the children to make up their own lullaby, perhaps by incorporating their name or the name of a special baby into the lyrics. Ask them to design and, if time permits, make simple instruments that will produce soft sounds. For instance, sand could be used instead of dried peas in a simple shaker.

## A Jigsaw Name Game

**RESOURCES:** thin card; scissors; paper; pencils; crayons

Discuss first names with the children. Show them how names can be split into syllables. Tell them that they are going to make a jigsaw of their name with one piece of the jigsaw for each syllable of their first name. Children who have only one syllable in their name will make a single card. They should think about their design first and make the cards attractive. Discuss the designs, then make the jigsaws. You could let the children go on to devise a game which uses the cards, or take out the single-syllable names and play the game that follows.

**RESOURCES:** two skipping-ropes; polysyllable name cards as made on page 90

Divide the children into small groups. Give each group a base so that the groups are equidistant from each other and from a circle (made from the skipping-ropes) in the centre of the floor. Give each group the first syllable of a name. The circle contains a large pile of syllables to complete the names. At a given signal, one member of each group runs round the circle, then searches in the pile for the syllable(s) which will complete their group's name. This is taken back to the group and they have finished when the entire group is standing up holding the completed name. Repeat the game several times so that everybody has a turn. Then add up the scores to find the overall winner.

## EXTENSION ACTIVITY

**RESOURCES:** items that are used to celebrate a baby's naming ceremony; paper; pencils; crayons; felt-tips; scissors; glue; paper plates; assorted junk modelling resources

Show the children the items that are given to celebrate a baby's naming ceremony, such as a card, a money box, or commemorative crockery. Help them to evaluate the items before going on to design and make their own.

# Zacchaeus

## Luke 19:1–10

Jesus went on into Jericho and was passing through. There was a chief tax collector there named Zacchaeus, who was rich. He was trying to see who Jesus was, but he was a little man and could not see Jesus because of the crowd. So he ran ahead of the crowd and climbed a sycamore tree to see Jesus, who was going to pass that way. When Jesus came to that place, he looked up and said to Zacchaeus, 'Hurry down, Zacchaeus, because I must stay in your house today.'

Zacchaeus hurried down and welcomed him with great joy. All the people who saw it started grumbling, 'This man has gone as a guest to the home of a sinner!'

Zacchaeus stood up and said to the Lord, 'Listen, sir! I will give half my belongings to the poor, and if I have cheated anyone, I will pay back four times as much.'

Jesus said to him, 'Salvation has come to this house today, for this man, also, is a descendant of Abraham. The Son of Man came to seek and to save the lost.'

## NATIONAL CURRICULUM POINTER: DESIGNING/MAKING SKILLS

## AIM: To introduce the concept of Jesus as a Saviour

### INTRODUCTION

When preparing this assembly, ask a shorter member of staff to help you. Choose six children, one from each year group, and tell the children to sort themselves out into order of height with the shortest nearest you. Ask Year Six (the tallest children) to stand up. Then ask the previously warned member of staff to stand behind them. Tell the children standing near you to make a group, with the shortest at the back. Ask the shortest child if they can see the member of staff. The point of this exercise is that they can't. Suggest that the shortest child jumps up and down. Can they see the member of staff now? Ask the rest of the school how they think the problem could be solved without anyone moving.

Eventually the answer will be that the child needs to be made taller in some way. At this point, get everyone to sit down, and lead into the story of Zacchaeus.

### STORY

Everybody has to pay the government money, to help run the country. The money that is collected is called taxes. It is collected by people called tax collectors. It's a bit unfair, but many people don't like tax collectors. In Jesus' time, there was one tax collector in Jericho whom everybody hated. He was called Zacchaeus. People hated him because they thought he cheated them and asked them for more taxes than they really owed. Zacchaeus had heard all about Jesus and wanted to see him when he was passing through Jericho. Unfortunately for Zacchaeus, lots of people had the same idea and the streets were crowded the day Jesus arrived. Now Zacchaeus was a very short man and he couldn't see a thing over the crowds' heads. **(Remind the children how the shortest child could not see the member of staff.)** He hadn't got a chair to stand on, he couldn't find a ladder, so he climbed a tree. Nobody noticed what he had done except for Jesus, who stopped under the tree and said, 'Hurry down, Zacchaeus, because I must stay in your house today.' Zacchaeus was very excited and quickly climbed down the tree. He took Jesus to his house and made him feel very welcome. The rest of the crowd followed and when they saw what was happening they began to complain and mutter. They said, 'Why does a good man like Jesus want to go and stay with a nasty man like Zacchaeus?' Zacchaeus knew what they were thinking and stood up in front of them all. He said, 'I will give half of everything I have to the poor, and if I have cheated anyone, I will pay them back four times as much.' Jesus said, 'That's a good thing to do. You've shown everyone you've changed and that you're sorry for the wrong things you've done. I came into the world to find people who were lost in their badness and help them to change.'

## PRAYERS

### A Responsorial Prayer based on Psalm 106:1–3

Explain that you are going to lead the children in a responsorial prayer. First teach the response, telling the children to repeat it after you several times, before trying it on their own. Explain that you will say a sentence of prayer and, when you stop, they will answer with the response.

The response is 'We give thanks to the Lord.'

---

'Dear Lord, you are good to us.
'We give thanks to the Lord.'
You will always be there for us.
'We give thanks to the Lord.'
You have done so many great things.
'We give thanks to the Lord.'
You have told us that if we obey you we will be happy.
'We give thanks to the Lord.'
Help us to do the right thing.
Amen

---

### Thinking Prayer

Tell the children to close their eyes and, just for a moment, think silently about something they have done wrong that they would like to say sorry for. After a brief silence say, 'Please forgive us, Lord, for the things we have done wrong and help

us to put them right. Amen'

Follow up this assembly, enabling the children to practise designing and making skills by using the most appropriate activities for your group from the selection below.

## ACTIVITIES

### A Moving Picture to Evaluate

RESOURCES: photocopiable sheets (Moving Picture and Moving Picture Evaluation Sheet); paper; card; scissors; glue; sticky tape; paints; brushes; crayons; felt-tips; pencils

Use the photocopiable sheet (Moving Picture) to help the children make a moving picture of Zacchaeus climbing up and down the tree. This method uses a simple tab mechanism to move the character. It can be made from different weights of paper or card, each of which will change the durability and effectiveness of the finished item. Key Stage Two children could use the Moving Picture Evaluation Sheet to help them consider the suitability of the material and method of making the picture. During this activity, opportunities will arise to remember the story and how Jesus changed the life of Zacchaeus.

### A Design Brief

RESOURCES: selection of suitable materials, which might include modelling material, cardboard, pipe cleaners, newspaper, empty boxes; glue; sticky tape; crêpe paper; paint; brushes; crayons (wax and pencil)

Tell the children that you want them to make a 3D model of a tree. Provide them with a variety of materials and discuss how they might be used to make a tree. For instance, corrugated card could be rolled and painted to make a trunk; pipe cleaners could be twisted and wrapped in crêpe paper to make branches or twigs, or modelling material could be shaped into a tree and painted after drying. Suggest that the children make a diagram of their design before starting to make their tree. As they work, you may have the opportunity to refresh their memory about the tree Zacchaeus climbed and what happened to him afterwards.

# A Board Game

**RESOURCES:** photocopiable sheet
(Board Game); selection of board games;
paper; card; scissors; glue; sticky tape;
paints; brushes; crayons; felt-tips; pencils

Discuss the board games the children
play. Show examples such as Snakes and Ladders,
and Ludo. Use the photocopiable sheet (Board
Game) to help the children make a simple board
game which helps to illustrate the story of
Zacchaeus and how Jesus helped him change his
life. Tell the children that you want them to think
of a board game of their own which would
remind them of the story of Zacchaeus. Divide
the group into pairs and tell them to work together. Suggest that they make a plan before they go
on to make the final game. When each pair has
completed their game, pass the games around and
let everybody have a go at playing someone else's
game. They could go on to evaluate each game
and choose a group favourite.

# Marzipan Leaf

**RESOURCES:** leaves or pictures of
leaves; food colouring; marzipan; new
brushes; biscuits; fairy cakes; large sponge cake;
icing sugar; water; kitchen tools to model with, e.g.
rolling-pin, plastic knife

The concept behind this activity is to make a
marzipan leaf to remind you of the tree
Zacchaeus climbed to see Jesus. It would be a
good idea to collect leaves to copy, either pictures
or the real thing. For Key Stage Two children
you might like to try to find sycamore leaves
but younger children should be offered a simple
oval shape, such as a bay leaf. Discuss with the
children the necessity for good hygiene when
handling food. Be sure that they follow the rules
as they complete the project. Look at the colours
of the leaves and demonstrate how to colour
ready-made marzipan with food colouring. Give
each child a chunk of the coloured marzipan and
tell them to make it into a leaf shape. You may
have to prompt them to roll it out and sculpt it to
achieve the desired shape. It will be easier to work
the marzipan if the surface it is being rolled on is
dusted with icing sugar. Older children could
paint on the veins or leaf markings using food
colouring. When the leaves are finished, they must
be left to dry. The activity could be rounded off
by using the leaves to decorate a plain sweet biscuit or small fairy cake. Stick the leaf to the surface
with a blob of glacé icing. Younger children could
put all their leaves on a large sponge cake and then
have a slice each.

**Cut out along the thick black lines.
Then cut along the slit.
Thread Zacchaeus through the slit and
push the tab up and down to make
Zacchaeus climb the tree.**

1.  **Was the moving picture difficult to make?**

2.  **Did you think the instructions were easy to follow?**

3.  **Who do you think would enjoy playing with the picture?**

4.  **Do you think it would stand up to a lot of use?**

5.  **Do you think it was an effective way of showing Zacchaeus climbing up a tree?**

6.  **Can you think of a better way of making a moving picture?**

7.  **Can you think of some way of making the picture more durable?**

## parts sheet

## base board

Colour the two pictures to match exactly. Cut out the base board. Cut out the parts along the thick black lines. Each player has a base board and a set of parts. You may take it in turns to throw a dice. If you get a 1 you may put the top of the tree on your base board, and so on. The winner is the first to put all their parts on their base board.

History

# Florence Nightingale

## 1 Thessalonians 5:17

Pray at all times.

**NATIONAL CURRICULUM POINTER (KEY STAGE ONE):**
**AREAS OF STUDY—FAMOUS PERSONALITIES**
**NATIONAL CURRICULUM POINTER (KEY STAGE TWO):**
**STUDY UNIT—VICTORIAN BRITAIN**

**AIM: To introduce the importance of prayer**

## INTRODUCTION

**RESOURCES:** pictures or photographs of modern nurses

Show the children a picture or photograph of a nurse. Ask the children what the person in the picture does. Do they know where the person is likely to work? Do any of them know anyone who is a nurse? Tell the children that nurses have to spend some time training to do their job. Explain that many years ago there was no such thing as a trained nurse, until a very famous woman realized how important it was to have trained nurses.

## STORY

**RESOURCES:** an old book (hard-backed and leather-bound if possible); oil lamp or picture of an oil lamp; white apron; a length of bandage

*Tell the children that you are going to show them some items and you want them to try to name the person you are going to talk about. Show them the items in the following order: the old book; oil lamp or picture of an oil lamp; white apron; length of bandage. The children should guess that the name of the person is Florence Nightingale. If they don't know, tell them. Then go on to relate the following story, holding up the items as you mention them.*

Florence Nightingale was born in 1820 into a wealthy family. Florence did not go to school but her father gave her a good education at home. It was rare in Victorian times for girls to have the chance to learn like this. But Florence's father did not intend her studies to lead her to finding a job; he just wanted her to be able to become a good wife and mother. Florence often talked to God, and she believed he spoke to her. Florence wrote about her conversations with God in her journal. *(Hold up the old book.)* When she was sixteen she knew that God had asked her to do something special for him, but God hadn't told her exactly what he wanted her to do. Florence chose to go and help those who were poor and ill. This was work her parents could not object to, and Florence discovered she enjoyed helping people who were sick. All this time, Florence continued to talk to God and tried to find out what the special job was that he had for her.

Her parents realized that Florence was not going to settle down and become the wife and mother they had imagined, so they gave in and allowed her to spend three months in Germany learning about nursing. *(Hold up the white apron.)* Florence returned to England and was offered a job as Superintendent of a hospital that cared for women who were ill. It had taken Florence a long time to become a nurse.

Florence Nightingale is best known for the work she did in Scutari Hospital during the Crimean War. Florence was asked by a friend called Sidney Herbert to take a group of nurses out to Scutari to help look after the wounded soldiers. Florence and her nurses had to work extremely hard because the hospital was in a terrible state. The patients were hungry and cold. They weren't properly looked after. Florence argued with the army doctors who were in charge of the hospital. Eventually she won the argument and started to improve the hospital.

She organized teams to clean the hospital, and to nurse the soldiers properly. *(Hold up the length of bandage.)* She even got people back in England involved in sending equipment out to Scutari to help. It was while Florence was nursing the soldiers at Scutari that she became known as 'The Lady with the Lamp'. There was no electricity in the hospital and every night Florence walked around it carrying her lamp so that she could see her way. *(Hold up the oil lamp.)* She spoke to every soldier and often stopped to comfort dying soldiers. The patients loved her so much that some said she was a saint. Everybody knew about Florence Nightingale and her tremendous work at Scutari, and the way she had made nursing seem a respectable profession for women. Florence continued to talk to God about her life, and she felt God was guiding her in what she did.

The Crimean War ended in 1856 but by now Florence was not well; she had worked hard in Scutari. She came back to England and wrote a book about nursing. The people in England were so impressed with what she had done in the Crimean War that they raised enough money to start a Nightingale School of Nursing so that women could be trained to nurse in the way Florence had shown them. The school opened in 1860. Florence Nightingale died in 1910, having spent her life listening to God and trying to obey him.

 **PRAYERS**

## A Responsorial Prayer

Explain that you are going to lead the children in a responsorial prayer. First teach the response, telling the children to repeat it after you several times before trying it on their own. Explain that you will say a sentence of prayer and when you stop they will answer with the response.

The response is, 'Please be near them.'

**Dear God,**
**When nurses are tired and weary,**
**'Please be near them.'**
**When nurses have difficult jobs to do,**
**'Please be near them.'**
**When nurses have to work at night or**
**early in the morning,**
**'Please be near them.'**
**Thank you, God, for nurses and the way they**
**care for people who are ill.**
**'Please be near them.' Amen**

## A Prayer for the Sick

This prayer focuses on the children and adults in your group who are not well. You will need to know the names beforehand. If you are dealing with a larger group you could ask each class teacher to mention the names of the children in their class at the appropriate moment in the prayer.

**Dear God,**
**We are thinking of adults who are not with us today**
**because they are not very well.**
(At this point, mention by name the adults known to you who are ill.)
**We miss them and ask you to be close to them.**
**We are thinking of children who are not with us**
**today because they are not very well.**
(At this point, mention by name the children who are ill.)
**We miss them and ask you to be close to them.**
**Please help those who are looking after the people**
**we have mentioned. Please show us if there is a**
**way in which we can help these people who are ill.**
**Amen**

It may be appropriate to follow up this prayer by sending a letter, a get-well card or a simple present to someone who has been mentioned.

Follow up this assembly, enabling the children to think about Florence Nightingale and Victorian Britain by using the most appropriate activities for your group from the selection suggested.

## ACTIVITIES

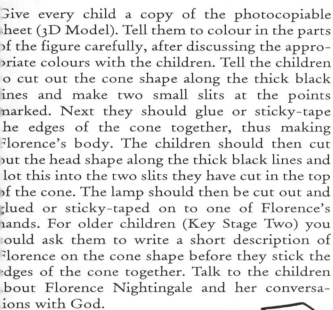

### 3D Model of Florence Nightingale

**RESOURCES:** photocopiable sheet (3D Model); scissors; crayons; glue or sticky tape; pencils

Give every child a copy of the photocopiable sheet (3D Model). Tell them to colour in the parts of the figure carefully, after discussing the appropriate colours with the children. Tell the children to cut out the cone shape along the thick black lines and make two small slits at the points marked. Next they should glue or sticky-tape the edges of the cone together, thus making Florence's body. The children should then cut out the head shape along the thick black lines and slot this into the two slits they have cut in the top of the cone. The lamp should then be cut out and glued or sticky-taped on to one of Florence's hands. For older children (Key Stage Two) you could ask them to write a short description of Florence on the cone shape before they stick the edges of the cone together. Talk to the children about Florence Nightingale and her conversations with God.

### Missing Words

**RESOURCES:** photocopiable sheet (Missing Words/Bookmark,); pencils; crayons

Give each child a copy of the photocopiable sheet (Missing Words/Bookmark). Read the sheet through with the children, putting in the missing words verbally as you go. Tell the children to try to complete the sheet for themselves. When the missing words have been filled in, the children could colour in the pictures around the text.

### Bookmark

**RESOURCES:** photocopiable sheet (Missing Words/Bookmark); card; crayons; paint; pencils; scissors; wool

Give each child the picture of Florence Nightingale from the photocopiable sheet (Missing Words/Bookmark) and tell them to colour it in. As they work, discuss with the children the life of Florence Nightingale and how she became a nurse. Stress the importance of prayer in her life. Discuss the advances Florence made in the care of the sick and the effect this has had on modern life. The children should then cut out the figure and stick it on to a piece of card (15 cm x 7 cm). On the back of the card they could write, 'Florence Nightingale 1820–1910'. They may like to add a short prayer thanking God for the life of Florence Nightingale. To finish the bookmark, the children could make a simple tassel from the wool and use it to decorate their bookmark.

### Prayer Scrapbook

**RESOURCES:** a scrapbook; paper; glue; reproduction Victorian 'scraps'; magazines

Discuss how wealthy Victorian ladies very rarely went out to work. Explain that they spent much of their time embroidering, reading, arranging flowers, painting pictures, visiting friends or making 'scrap' books. Contrast this with the life of poorer Victorian women who had to work very hard. Remind the children about Florence Nightingale and her dependence on prayer. Tell them that one of the things she may have done when she lived at home with her parents was to make a 'scrap' book. Ask each child to write a simple prayer and decorate it either with reproduction Victorian 'scraps' or with pictures cut from modern magazines. When all the prayers are complete, use them to form the basis for a prayer scrapbook. To finish the book, decorate the cover.

### Floor Game

**RESOURCES:** A4 sheets of paper; felt-tips; thin card; glue; scissors; dice; counters made from the figure of Florence Nightingale on the photocopiable sheets (Missing Words/Bookmark; Floor Game)

Tell the children that you are going to make a giant floor game about the life of Florence Nightingale. First of all, they will each need to make a counter in the shape of Florence Nightingale. Give each child a copy of the photocopiable sheet (Missing Words/Bookmark) to colour in, cut out and stick on to thin card. Next, display, where everybody can see it, the list on the Floor Game photocopiable sheet.

Organize your group so that each child copies a statement on to a piece of paper. If you have a small group, some children may have to do more than one. If you have a larger group, some children could decorate blank papers with pictures showing scenes from Florence Nightingale's life. You need to ensure that you add a blank paper between each of the statements listed above. When all the papers are completed, take the children to a large area where you have room to play the game in safety. Put the 'Start' paper where you want the children to start and lay out the papers around the space, ending with the 'Finish' paper. Split the children into groups of two or three and let each group in turn start the game by throwing the dice. The children move their counters round the course according to the throw of the dice and the instructions they land on. The winner is the first child to reach the finish.

## Comparison Pictures

**RESOURCES:** appropriate resource books; photocopiable sheet (Comparison); pencils; crayons; paper

Remind the children of the way sick people were looked after before Florence Nightingale trained nurses. Give each child a copy of the photocopiable sheet (Comparison). Tell them that on the first half of their sheet they will find a picture of a Victorian nurse at the time of Florence

Nightingale. They may like to refer to the resource books to help them colour it in correctly. On the other half of the sheet they should draw a picture of a modern nurse. They could use appropriate resource books to make sure that they draw an accurate picture. Discuss with the children how Florence regularly prayed to God and decided that her life should not be spent idly but, rather, in looking after the poor and sick. Older children (Key Stage Two) might like to extend this activity by thinking about the changes in nursing care over the years. They could compile a list, then use the list to write a 'thank you' prayer for progress in the world of medicine.

## ✚ EXTENSION ACTIVITY

Discuss with the children the changes that have already occurred in their lives, such as a growing ability to look after themselves. They could also think about their ambitions and hopes, such as which secondary school they would like to attend. The children could make a very simple booklet from paper and card which they might like to keep as a prayer journal, just as Florence Nightingale did.

# FLORENCE NIGHTINGALE

Florence _____ was born in _____ . Her parents were very _____ . Florence often talked to _____ . She was sure he wanted _____ to do something very _____ . Florence was allowed to go to _____ to learn about _____ . When she came back to England, she _____ a job as a _____ in a hospital. When the _____ War began, Florence went to _____ to help the _____ . She took a group of _____ with her. Florence became known as the _____ with the _____ because she _____ round the wards of the _____ carrying a _____ . After the _____ War Florence went back to _____ and wrote a _____ about _____ . She died in _____ .

**1**

**2**

## FLOOR GAME

1820 Born . . . . . . . . . . . . . . . . . . . . . . . . . . . . . . . Start

Florence realizes God has a special task for her . . . . . . . Go on 2

Visited the poor and sick . . . . . . . . . . . . . . . . . . . . . Go on 1

Allowed to work at Kaiserswerth Institution, Germany. . . . Go on 1

Florence kept a journal. . . . . . . . . . . . . . . . . . . . . . . Go on 1

Became Superintendent of Nurses at Middlesex Hospital . Go on 1

1854 Crimean War starts. . . . . . . . . . . . . . . . . . . . . . Go back 2

Arrived in Scutari; found terrible conditions . . . . . . . . . . Go back 3

Florence talked to God . . . . . . . . . . . . . . . . . . . . . . . Go on 1

In Scutari, argued with army officers . . . . . . . . . . . . . . Go back 2

In Scutari, relief supplies from England arrive. . . . . . . . . Go on 2

Florence becomes known as 'The Lady with the Lamp' . . . Go on 2

1856 Crimean War ends. . . . . . . . . . . . . . . . . . . . . . . Go on 2

1856 Received personal thanks from Queen Victoria. . . . . Go on 3

Wrote Notes on Nursing . . . . . . . . . . . . . . . . . . . . . . . Go on 1

1860 Nightingale School of Nursing begun . . . . . . . . . . . Go on 2

1910 Florence dies. . . . . . . . . . . . . . . . . . . . . . . . . . Finish

# Saint Augustine

## Mark 16:15

He said to them, 'Go throughout the whole world and preach the gospel to the whole human race.'

**NATIONAL CURRICULUM POINTER (KEY STAGE ONE):**
**AREAS OF STUDY—FAMOUS PERSONALITIES**
**NATIONAL CURRICULUM POINTER (KEY STAGE TWO):**
**STUDY UNIT—ANGLO-SAXONS IN BRITAIN**

## AIM: To introduce the idea of evangelism and missionaries

### INTRODUCTION

**RESOURCES:**

photocopiable sheet (Saint Augustine) used as OHP slides

Discuss monks and nuns with the children. Do any of them know what a monk or a nun is? What does a monk or a nun do? Show the first OHP slide and tell the children that some people choose to dedicate their lives to God nowadays. Some women do this by becoming nuns and some men do this by becoming monks. They spend their lives talking to God, worshipping God and trying to do what he wants. Discuss with the children the lives of modern-day monks and nuns and how some work in hospitals or schools. Explain that there have always been people who wanted to dedicate their lives to God by being monks or nuns. Show the second OHP slide and tell the children that this is a picture of Saint Augustine, who was a very famous monk in Anglo-Saxon times.

### STORY

**RESOURCES:** OHP slides from photocopiable sheet (St Augustine)

*Show the OHP slide of Saint Augustine and tell the following story.*

Long ago, a young monk called Gregory was walking through a market in Rome. He saw a group of slaves being sold. They looked very different from most of the people Gregory knew. They had fair hair and skin. Gregory asked where the slaves came from. He was told that they were Angles. Angles were a heathen people who had not heard about the Christian God and lived in what we now call Britain. Gregory said that the slaves were so fair they should be called angels, not Angles.

Gregory never forgot the heathen slaves in the market-place. When he became Pope, he asked an old friend, Augustine, who was also a monk, to go and tell the Angles all about God and Christianity. Gregory told Augustine to take a group of monks with him to help. Gregory knew that he was giving Augustine a very difficult job because the Angles lived on an island a long way from Rome and were supposed to be very rough and unfriendly.

Augustine and his monks set off. They travelled across what we now call Europe and eventually reached the coast of France. The nearer they got to the sea, the more they heard terrible stories about the Angles—how unfriendly they were and what awful things they did. The monks with Augustine believed the stories and refused to leave France to travel to Britain. Despite all Augustine's efforts, his monks wouldn't move and he felt that the only thing he could do was to go back to his friend, Pope Gregory, in Rome.

Pope Gregory felt it was such an important mission that Augustine must go on. So he tried to help by giving Augustine a letter for his monks that would reassure them about how important their job was. Augustine returned to his monks and they agreed to set off to cross the sea to Britain. They landed in Kent in spring AD597.

At this time, Britain was divided into a number of small kingdoms and Ethelbert was the king of Kent. He was married to a Christian princess called Bertha. King Ethelbert sent messages to Augustine and his monks to say that he would come and meet them to hear what they wanted to say. A few days after Augustine had landed, King Ethelbert and his friends went to meet Augustine, but King Ethelbert wasn't sure that he could trust Augustine, so he insisted that they meet in the open air. At that meeting Augustine spoke to King Ethelbert about God and what Pope Gregory had asked him to do. Ethelbert was impressed with what Augustine told him and offered to help the monks by allowing them to use his wife Bertha's church near the city of Canterbury. Bertha had a church because she was already a Christian and worshipped God with her friends in Saint Martin's church.

Augustine and his monks set off to walk to Saint Martin's, singing prayers and carrying a silver cross.

By Christmas AD597, King Ethelbert and many of his friends had become Christians. Augustine was able to send messengers back to Pope Gregory to tell him how well their mission was going and asking for more monks to help with the mission.

Show the OHP slide of modern monks and nuns and explain that nowadays monks and nuns still travel to other countries to tell people about God.

## PRAYERS

### A Responsorial Prayer

Explain that you are going to lead the children in a responsorial prayer. First teach the response. When they have learnt it, explain that you will say a sentence of the prayer and, when you stop, they will answer with the response.

The response is 'Help us to share your love.'

---

**Dear God,
As we remember Saint Augustine,
'Help us to share your love.'
As we remember what a difficult mission he had,
'Help us to share your love.'
As we remember Augustine's courage,
'Help us to share your love.'
As we go out from here,
'Help us to share your love.'
Amen**

## A Thinking Prayer

Tell the children to be quiet for a few moments and think about modern missionaries who go to other lands to share God's love. If you know a missionary, it might be appropriate to tell the children about them and their work at this point. After a brief silence, say, 'Thank you, God, for missionaries who share your love with other people. Amen'

Follow up this assembly, enabling the children to think about Saint Augustine and the coming of Christianity to Britain by using the most appropriate activities for your group from the selection suggested.

## ACTIVITIES

### Illuminated Initial

**RESOURCES:** photocopiable sheet (Illuminated Initial); crayons; felt-tips; pencils; squared paper; coloured inks; photograph or picture of an illuminated manuscript

Discuss with the children the lives of monks and how they lived. Explain that about a thousand years ago there were no printing presses and monks, who were better educated than other people, copied books by hand. The books they copied were mainly religious books and they used to decorate the first letters on each page. Show the children the photograph or picture and discuss the intricacies of the illuminated letters. Give each child a copy of the photocopiable sheet (Illuminated Initial), which shows A for Augustine, and tell them to colour it in carefully. The children might like to extend the activity by creating their own illuminated initial for their first name, their second name or both.

### Letter from Pope Gregory

**RESOURCES:** paper; pencils; crayons; felt-tips

Remind the children of the story they heard in assembly and how Augustine sent a message to his friend, Pope Gregory, asking for more help with the mission. Tell the children that Gregory replied and sent more monks to help. Pope Gregory also sent a letter to King Ethelbert to congratulate him on becoming a Christian. Tell the children that you want them to write the letter that Pope Gregory might have sent. When the letters are complete, the children could copy them out before illuminating the first letter and decorating the border around the text.

## Spelling Tig

**RESOURCES:** two sets of letter cards of different colours, one set that spells the name 'Augustine' and one set that spells the name 'Ethelbert'

Take the children to an open space where they can run around in safety. Choose two children to be 'it'. Give one child the set of letters that spells Augustine and the other child the set of letters that spells Ethelbert. Explain that these two children are the catchers and every time they catch somebody they will give them a letter. The game will end when the two catchers have no more cards left. At the end of the game you might like to challenge the children to get together into groups all of the same colour card and try to spell out the names. Remind the children that Augustine came to tell King Ethelbert about God. If you have a smaller group of children, use only one set of cards.

## Monk Collage

**RESOURCES:** paper; a variety of collage materials; glue; scissors; pencils; resource books about Anglo-Saxon Britain

Remind the children of the story, particularly the part when Augustine landed on the coast of Kent. Discuss Anglo-Saxon Britain with the children and talk to them about Augustine and his monks, who came as missionaries to bring the message of God's love to the Anglo-Saxons. Tell them to design a large picture of Augustine and his monks landing in Britain. Suggest that the children collage the picture, making sure that they are using the right colours etc. by checking in the appropriate resource books.

## Walk for Evangelism

**RESOURCES:** four posters with the words 'Rome', 'France', 'Isle of Thanet', 'Canterbury'; cardboard cross on a garden cane

Before the activity, place the four posters around a large area. The positioning of the posters will govern the route along which you walk. Take the children into the large area and remind them that in Anglo-Saxon times there were no forms of motorized transport. Augustine and his monks had to travel mostly on foot. Even the boat that they crossed the Channel in would have been no more than a simple sailing vessel. Explain to the children that you are going to 'act out' Augustine's walk. Choose one child to carry the cross. Next, ask the children if they can remember where the journey started. They should say, 'Rome' and can then be asked to look for the

'Rome' poster. Gather all the children together at the poster and tell them to form into a procession behind the cross as, together, you walk round the large area looking for the next poster in the sequence. During the course of the walk you could point out to the children that the monks sang as they walked, and ask the children to suggest a favourite hymn or praise song they might sing. As you visit each poster, remind the children of the story of Saint Augustine's mission to Anglo-Saxon Britain. After the walk you may find an opportunity to discuss with the children modern-day walks that Christians go on to spread the love of God to others.

## Story Sequence

**RESOURCES:** photocopiable sheet (Story Sequence); paper; glue; scissors; crayons; pencils

Give each child a copy of the photocopiable sheet (Story Sequence). Explain that the sheet shows a series of pictures which retell the story of Saint Augustine's mission. If you have enough time, get the children to colour the pictures in at this point. You might wish to emphasize the use of the correct colours. Next, explain that the pictures are in the wrong order on the sheet. Tell the children to cut the pictures out and stick them on a separate piece of paper in the correct order. As the children work, talk about the story and explain that Saint Augustine was an evangelist, someone who came to tell other people about God.

**Modern
monks
and nuns**

**Monks of the
year AD597**

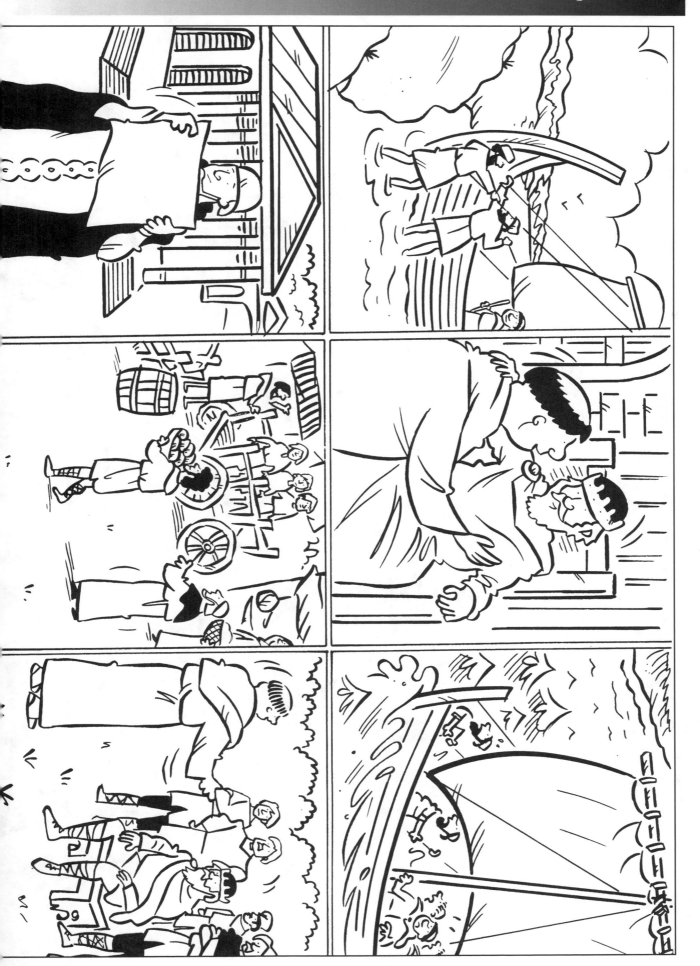

# Victorian Sunday Schools

## Deuteronomy 6:5–9

Love the Lord your God with all your heart, with all your soul, and with all your strength. Never forget these commands that I am giving you today. Teach them to your children. Repeat them when you are at home and when you are away, when you are resting and when you are working. Tie them on your arms and wear them on your foreheads as a reminder. Write them on the door-posts of your houses and on your gates.

**NATIONAL CURRICULUM POINTER (KEY STAGE ONE):**
**AREAS OF STUDY—PAST EVENTS**
**NATIONAL CURRICULUM POINTER (KEY STAGE TWO):**
**STUDY UNIT—VICTORIAN BRITAIN**

## AIM: To introduce the idea of Christians learning about their faith

## INTRODUCTION

Ask the children if any of their older brothers or sisters have a paper-round. Go on to discuss when they do their paper-round and if doing the paper-round means that they do not have to go to school. Obviously you should receive the answer that all children have to go to school, whether or not they have a paper-round. Ask if the children know at what age you start school and at what age you leave school. Go on to explain that it has not always been like this. In fact, many years ago children did not have to go to school.

## STORY

**RESOURCES:** Make four OHP slides using the pictures on the photocopiable sheet (Victorian Sunday Schools)

**Tell the following story using the OHP slides to illustrate it.**

When Victoria became Queen (show OHP 1) there were no schools as we know them today. Children of wealthy parents were either taught at home by a tutor or a governess, or went to a school where their parents had to pay for their education. But poor children had to work to earn money to help their families. Many children worked long hours in coal mines. Some of them were actually chained to coal wagons which they had to move through the long underground passages of the mines. Other children were employed as 'climbing boys', which means that they worked for a chimney-sweep, who made them climb up the inside of chimneys with brushes to clean them. Some children worked in factories (show OHP 2). The children worked such long hours that there was no spare time they could use to go to school. The only day that most poor people had to themselves was a Sunday. Some people realized that children needed to learn to read and write, do sums and learn about God. They decided to provide free schools on a Sunday so that the poor children could learn on their day off. These Sunday schools were often called 'ragged schools' because the poor children who went to them did not have nice clothes or shoes. The lessons in these schools were very simple. The children learnt to read and write a little, and do simple sums, and they also learnt about the Christian faith. Eventually the government decided that education was very important and by 1880 it was compulsory for all children under ten to be educated (show OHP 3). Today we are very lucky because there are good, free schools for everybody, and children do not have to work long hours in horrible conditions to earn money for their families. But some children still learn on a Sunday (show OHP 4). They don't go to schools, but to church groups, where they are taught about the Christian faith.

## A Personalized School Prayer

The prayer below has blanks which you can fill in with things
that are particularly relevant to the children in your group.

---

**Dear God,**
**Thank you for _____ school.**
**Thank you for the things we learn there, especially _____.**
**Thank you for the fun we have at school.**
**Thank you for our teachers and all the adults who help us in our school.**
**Thank you for the equipment we use to help us learn,**
**especially _____.**
**Thank you for the opportunity to go to school.**
**Help us to make good use of the time we spend there.**
**Amen**

---

**Dear God,**
**Sunday is a special day when we can learn about you.**
**Help us to learn about you throughout the week.**
**Help us to remember you as we walk through your world.**
**Help us to find time to read your word in the Bible.**
**When we talk to you, help us to listen carefully.**
**Thank you that you love and care for us.**
**Amen**

---

Follow up this assembly, enabling the children to think about
Victorian Sunday Schools by using the most appropriate activities
for your group from the selection below.

## ACTIVITIES

### A Bible Verse to Learn

**RESOURCES:** paper; pencils; Bibles for older children (Key Stage Two); a Bible verse written out for younger children (Key Stage One); crayons; felt-tips; self-adhesive stars

Discuss with the children the way that Victorian children had to learn and recite verses of the Bible. Teach older children how to look up a verse in the Bible (for this activity, try Deuteronomy 6:5–6). For younger children, copy out the verse (try using just one phrase from the verse, such as 'Love the Lord your God'). Explain to the children that they are going to learn this verse. One way in which Victorian children might have learnt a Bible verse would have been to chant it aloud together. Read the verse to the children, then tell them that you are all going to chant the verse together. After you have chanted the verse, you could explain that another way Victorian children might have learnt would have been to copy the verse several times in their best handwriting. Explain that, although you are not going to ask them to copy the verse lots of times, you would like them to copy it once and then decorate the page. When the Bible verses are completed, give the children an opportunity to learn the verse quietly by themselves. Then ask for volunteers to recite the verse out loud. Tell the children that when they have recited the verse to the rest of the children, they can have a star to stick on their copy of the verse. Remind the children that although they don't have to learn Bible verses, one way that they can find out about God is to read their Bible.

# Then and Now Model

**RESOURCES:** photocopiable sheet
(Model) on thin card; pencils; crayons;
scissors; felt-tips; appropriate resource books

Discuss the differences between a poor Victorian
child and a modern child. Talk about the differences in clothes, footwear and cleanliness. Give
each child a copy of the photocopiable sheet
(Model) photocopied on to thin card. Tell the
children that one set of clothes is for the Victorian
child and the children must go and look up what
sort of colours would be most appropriate. When
they have found out the information, they
should colour in the Victorian set of clothes. The
children can then colour in the modern clothes,
using their favourite colours or thinking about
their own favourite outfit. Finally, the children
need to colour in the model of the child. The
clothes and the model can then be cut out. You
might go on to create two backgrounds, one of a
ragged school and one of a modern school.
Discuss with the children how good it is that they
have the opportunity to go to school and also are
able to learn about God in church groups. You
could then ask the children to choose which set of
clothes to dress their model in, before placing it
against the appropriate background.

# What's the Word?

**RESOURCES:** a set of cards each
showing one letter from a word, one set
of cards for each team

In order to play the game, you will need to decide
on one word that each team will find. You could
use 'foreheads' and 'doorposts' from the Bible
reference. Whatever words you choose, it is
important that there are the same number of
letters in each team's word. Before playing the
game, you will need to hide the sets of letters
around the room. Then, to play the game, divide
the children into teams and tell each team what
their word is. Challenge the teams to find the
letters which make up their word. When all the
letters are found, the team must stand up. Each
team member should hold up one letter and the
team must stand in the correct order to spell their
word. The winner is the first team to create their
word. After the game, discuss with the children
how, in a Victorian school, spelling would have
been learnt by chanting the names of the letters.
Challenge each team to chant the letters of their
words, saying, for instance, 'F, O, R, E, H, E, A,
D, S, spells foreheads'.

# Hymn Singing

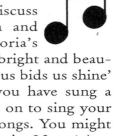

Have a hymn-singing session. Discuss
the hymns that were written and
became popular during Victoria's
reign. You might use 'All things bright and beautiful' (Junior Praise No. 6) or 'Jesus bids us shine'
(Junior Praise No. 128). After you have sung a
selection of Victorian hymns, go on to sing your
favourite modern action praise songs. You might
use 'My God is so big' (Junior Praise No. 169) or
'He brought me to his banqueting house' (Junior
Praise No. 73). You might like to extend this
activity by going on to learn about the life of one
of the famous Victorian hymn-writers.

# Going to School Board Game

**RESOURCES:** photocopiable sheet
(Board Game); scissors; felt-tips; crayons;
pencils; dice

Discuss with the children how difficult it
was for poor Victorian children to go to school.
Explain that there were many problems which
could prevent them from attending school. Give
each child a copy of the photocopiable sheet
(Board Game) and explain that they are going to
make a board game in which the winner is the
person who manages to get to school first. Tell
the children to colour in and cut out the
Victorian children on the sheet; these will be the
counters for the game. The children will then
need to cut out the stands for these figures, so
that they can stand up. The board should then be
coloured in. When all the games are complete,
divide the children into pairs and let them play
the game. Tell the pairs to swap over and play each
other's games. The children may like to take their
games home and play them with their families.

# Victorian Quiz Dice

**RESOURCES:** photocopiable sheet
(Quiz Dice) on thin card; pencils; scissors; glue
or sticky tape; felt-tips

Remind the children about how
hard life was for poor children during Victoria's reign. Explain that
sometimes the whole family would work together
at home, making things such as matchboxes. The
family had to work very long hours because they
earned so little money for each box. Sometimes
the younger children were so tired that they
would fall asleep in the middle of making a box.
Their parents would have to wake them up
because the work needed to be done, otherwise
the family would not have enough money for

food. Remind the children that nowadays life is not as hard as it was in Victorian England and we must remember to thank God for all the good things we have. Tell the children that they are going to make just one box, but it will be a special box to help them remember facts about the reign of Queen Victoria. Give each child a copy of the photocopiable sheet (Quiz Dice). The photocopiable sheet contains the net of a dice and three questions and answers you might use on it. You can either let the children write the given questions and answers on their net or make up more questions and answers yourself so that every child's dice has a different set. You could even suggest that the children make up their own questions and answers. The first thing the children need to do is to write their questions and answers on the net. It is important that the answer is always on the opposite face to its question, so the net is marked accordingly. Once the questions and answers are on the net, tell the children to cut out the dice net and stick it together carefully. Next, explain how they can roll the quiz dice and find either an answer or a question on the uppermost face when the dice stops. If the children find a question, they must answer it. If they find an answer, they should try to work out what the question must have been. They can check if they are correct by looking on the opposite face of the dice.

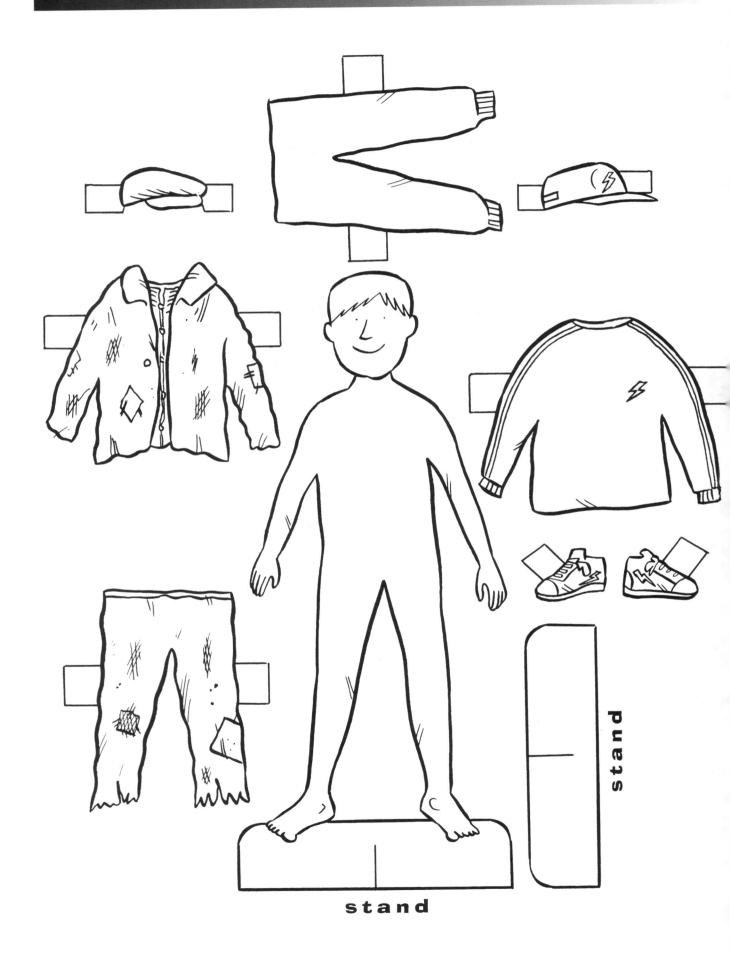

stand

stand

Throw a 6 to **START**

Got new boots. Go on three.

Dad lost his job. Go back two.

Too tired after work in factory. Go back two.

School opens in next village. Go on one.

Had to look after the baby. Go back four.

Mum found a penny. Go on two.

Didn't make enough matches. Had to work longer. Go back four.

Dad got a new job. Go on two.

Mum ill. Had to look after other kids. Go back two.

Throw a six to get into school.

**SCHOOL**

**QUIZ DICE**

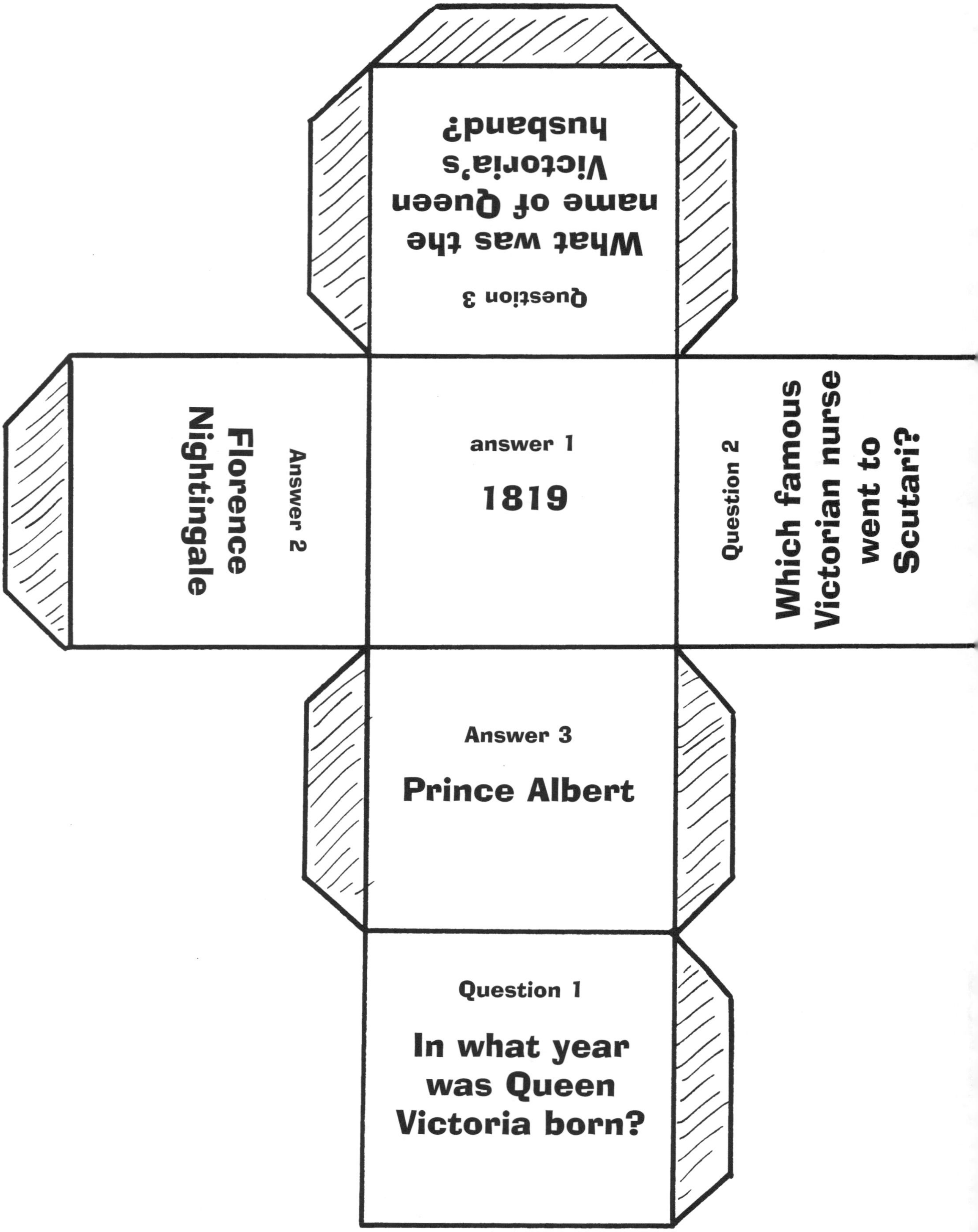

Question 3
What was the name of Queen Victoria's husband?

Answer 2
Florence Nightingale

answer 1
1819

Question 2
Which famous Victorian nurse went to Scutari?

Answer 3
Prince Albert

Question 1
In what year was Queen Victoria born?

# The Blitz and Coventry Cathedral

## Ephesians 4:32

Instead, be kind and tender-hearted to one another, and forgive one another, as God has forgiven you through Christ.

**NATIONAL CURRICULUM POINTER (KEY STAGE ONE):**
**AREAS OF STUDY—PAST EVENTS**
**NATIONAL CURRICULUM POINTER (KEY STAGE TWO):**
**STUDY UNIT—BRITAIN SINCE 1930 (THE BLITZ)**

## AIM: To discuss the concept of forgiveness

## INTRODUCTION

**RESOURCES:** pictures or posters showing a variety of churches, places of worship and a cathedral (your nearest one if possible)

Show the children the pictures or posters of churches and places of worship. Discuss with them what these places are used for and by whom. Talk about the size of the buildings, how some are very small but others are very large, impressive buildings. Explain to the children that large towns called cities often have a cathedral. A cathedral is a very large church and is usually the main one in a group of churches. Tell the children about your nearest cathedral (or the one you have a picture of). Explain to the children that one British cathedral is famous because it was destroyed during World War II and was later rebuilt.

## STORY

**RESOURCES:** silhouettes from photocopiable sheet (The Blitz and Coventry Cathedral) copied on to separate OHP slides; red cellophane to back on to the cathedral silhouette so that the windows appear to have flames in them; an OHP

*Talk about the Blitz, how it got its name from the word 'Blitzkrieg', and for how long it continued during World War II. Put the two silhouettes of the cathedral together, one on top of the other so that the black one is on the top. Place both silhouettes on the OHP. Tell the children that this silhouette shows Coventry Cathedral on the night of 14 November 1940. Place the silhouette of the moon on the OHP and explain that it was a cold winter's night with a very bright moon.* The people of Coventry were nervous because they knew that this was the perfect night for the Germans to attempt to bomb the factories in their city. Coventry had already been bombed several times before. The people of Coventry knew what to do. The city was already in darkness; no light was allowed to appear anywhere. Where people had access to a bomb shelter, they had put emergency supplies in it—supplies such as candles, matches, blankets and food.

When the sirens sounded in Coventry at about 7.00 p.m. many adults had special jobs to do, such as being fire service volunteers or air raid wardens. Some adults were fire-watchers, whose job was to try to protect buildings from the fires that the bombs caused. Some fire-watchers were on the roof of Coventry Cathedral. The roof was worrying them because it was made from wood and lead and they knew that if a bomb crashed through the lead roof it would be almost impossible to put out the fire. Suddenly, the fire-watchers on the roof heard the sound of many aircraft overhead. *(Place the silhouette of the aircraft on the OHP.)* Before long, the planes started dropping their bombs. *(Place silhouette of bomb on OHP.)* The sound of the bombs dropping and the explosions caused by them made a terrible noise. The fire-watchers realized that this was a bad raid because they could also hear the rumble of buildings collapsing and they could see flames beginning to appear all around them. Several bombs hit the cathedral and, although they tried hard, the fire-watchers could not put the flames out. The cathedral burnt. **(Take off the top 'black' silhouette of the cathedral, leaving the one which shows the windows and doors, against a red background.)** The fire engines could not reach the building straightaway because of the damage the bombing was causing throughout the city. When fire engines did arrive, they tried to put the fire out, but after a while there was no more water for them to use because the water main had been destroyed. Soon the cathedral became a roofless shell.

Next morning the people of Coventry began moving around their city. They could not believe the terrible destruction the bombs had caused. In the ruined cathedral, one of the fire-watchers, Jock Forbes, saw that two of the old oak beams, which had been part of the roof, had fallen across each other. He tied them together as they were— the shape they made was that of a cross. Later that same morning a priest picked up three medieval nails from the ruins and turned them too into a cross. These crosses gave the people of Coventry hope, and they decided they would rebuild their city and its cathedral as soon as they could. Coventry now has a new cathedral which is linked to the ruins of the cathedral that was bombed. The crosses which were made the morning after the bombing have become very important to many Christians because the people of Coventry forgave the people who bombed their city. If you visit Coventry Cathedral nowadays you can see the ruins, and in the cathedral is a cross like the one made from the roof timbers. There is also an altar with the words 'Father Forgive' written on the wall behind it. Just like the people of Coventry, God wants us to forgive people who hurt us.

## PRAYERS

### Using a Photocopiable Sheet

**RESOURCES:** photocopiable sheet (Prayer); pencils (if completing this activity during the assembly); felt-tips and crayons will also be needed

Give each child a copy of the photocopiable sheet (Prayer). Ask the children to sit very still and quiet and look at the cross on their sheet while they think about the way God will always forgive us if we ask him to. Tell them to think about things that have upset them and how they must

try to forgive others just as they want God to forgive them. After a few moments of silence read the prayer on the photocopiable sheet (Prayer). Tell the children that they should complete the sheet now by adding their own prayers to it and colouring it in. Alternatively, you could let every child take the sheet back to their classroom to complete later.

## A Prayer about Forgiveness

Tell the children that every Friday, in the ruins of the old Coventry Cathedral, people recite a Litany of Reconciliation. A litany is where somebody says a sentence of prayer and everybody else replies with a response. Explain to the children that they are going to take part in a Litany of Forgiveness. Tell them that you will say a sentence of prayer and they will respond by saying, 'Please help us to forgive.'

---

**Dear God,
When our friends fall out with us,
'Please help us to forgive.'
When people call us names,
'Please help us to forgive.'
When somebody makes us cross,
'Please help us to forgive.'
When somebody pushes us
by mistake,
'Please help us to forgive.'
When we are feeling hurt
and angry,
'Please help us to forgive.'
Amen**

---

Follow up this assembly, enabling the children to think about the Blitz and Coventry Cathedral by using the most suitable activities for your group from the selection below.

## ACTIVITIES

### Silhouettes

**RESOURCES:** white paper; yellow and red paint; paintbrushes; water; black paper; scissors; glue; photocopiable sheet (The Blitz and Coventry Cathedral)

Discuss with the children the night Coventry Cathedral was destroyed and how the dark night sky must have been lit up by the bombs and the flames. Give each child a piece of white paper, a paintbrush, water, and yellow and red paint. To he children to paint the paper with yellow and red swirling patterns, sometimes adding extra water so that the colours blend to make orange. Show the children the photocopiable sheet (The Blitz and Coventry Cathedral) and explain what the silhouettes on the sheet are. Tell them that they should cut out the silhouettes and use them to create their own picture of the bombing of Coventry Cathedral on their painted sheet. When the pictures are complete, make a wall display of them and stretch across it a banner that says, 'Father Forgive'. Tell the children how Coventry Cathedral is now known across the world as a place that tries to bring nations into friendship with each other.

## 3D Model

**RESOURCES:** black pipe-cleaners; red, orange and yellow card; small, shallow cardboard boxes with lids (cheese boxes are ideal); glue; scissors; sticky tape; grey paint; permanent marker

Remind the children of the charred cross in Coventry Cathedral and its message of forgiveness. Give each child a small, shallow cardboard box with a lid, and tell them to paint the box grey. While the boxes dry, give each child some black pipe-cleaners and show them how to twist and shape them into a cross. Tell the children to cut out some flame shapes, a little bigger than their cross, from the coloured card. Once the boxes are dry, show the children how to make slits in the lid of their cardboard box through which to thread the flame shapes and the base of their pipe-cleaner cross. The cross should be placed through a central slit, while the flames should be arranged in a circular pattern around it. The children should then turn the lid of the box over, fold over the ends of the flames and the cross, and sticky-tape them firmly into place. The lid should then be put back on to the box and glued into place. The words 'Forgive one another' should be written with permanent marker around the edge of the box.

## Blackout Poster

**RESOURCES:** paper; pencils; felt-tips; crayons; appropriate resource books

Discuss the blackout with the children—why it was necessary and how it affected ordinary people. Talk about the Air Raid Precaution (ARP) Wardens whose job was to walk along the streets checking that everyone had followed the blackout rules. Explain that people could be fined if they showed a light from their windows or doors. Tell the children that the government issued posters to remind people of the blackout rules. If possible, find some examples of these posters in the resource books. Tell the children that you want them to look at the posters in the books, then design and make their own blackout poster. When the posters are complete, talk about the Blitz and how, although it was very hard, the people of Coventry forgave those who had bombed their city. Talk about how God wants us to try to forgive people who have hurt us.

## Shelter Race

**RESOURCES:** whistle; tables

Talk to the children about air raid shelters and how people had to shelter during an air raid. Remind them that it was important to get into the shelter quickly but safely. Explain that there were two sorts of air raid shelters—an Anderson shelter, which was used outside, and a Morrison shelter, which was used inside. Divide the children into teams of three or four. Designate one table to be the shelter for each group, making sure that the tables are well separated and in a safe area for the game to be played. Tell the children that, when the whistle is blown, they must imagine it is an air raid siren and they must get into their shelter as quickly and safely as possible. Stress that they must not push or jostle each other—it was important in an air raid to try to remain as calm as possible. Tell the children they may not come out until you blow the whistle again to signal the 'all clear'.

While the children are in their 'shelters' you might like to talk to them about what children did while they were in the shelters. Often people spent a long time in the shelters—they slept and ate there. Children who went into a shelter during school time often had to recite their times tables and do schoolwork while the raids continued. Discuss how frightening it must have been to be in a shelter while the bombs fell all around you. Talk about how people talked and prayed to God while they were in these shelters.

## Make Do and Mend

**RESOURCES:** a variety of materials that would normally be thrown away, e.g. cardboard tubes, junk mail, scraps of material etc; glue; sewing materials; scissors; pencils; felt-tips

Discuss with the children the way factories during World War II had to make guns, uniforms, tanks and aircraft rather than things like furniture, clothing, toys and comics. Explain that this meant that lots of things became difficult, if not impossible, to buy. People in Britain had to 'make do and mend'. They would often use something that nowadays we would throw away, to make a useful article.

*(continued on page 130)*

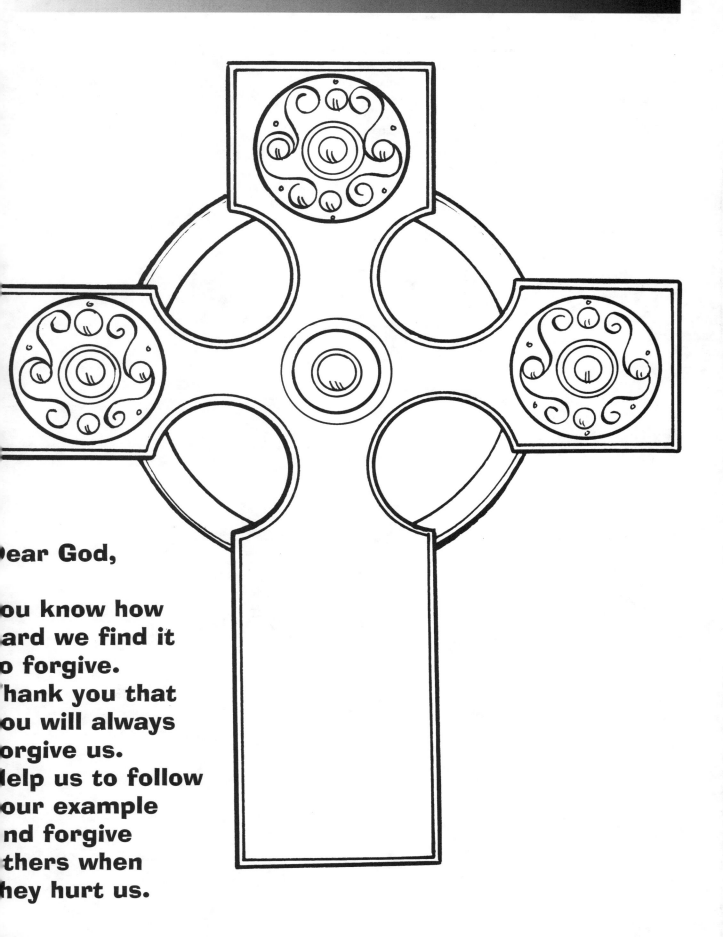

Dear God,

You know how hard we find it to forgive. Thank you that you will always forgive us. Help us to follow your example and forgive others when they hurt us.

Amen

Clothes would be carefully mended but, once outgrown, they would be passed on to a smaller child. Tell the children that you want them to make a useful item from the collection of junk materials you have provided. Depending on what you have collected, the children might make a pencil-holder, a notebook, a pincushion or a needle-case etc. Tell the children that sometimes, when we have done something wrong, we feel a bit like junk material; but, if we ask him, God will always forgive us and help us turn back into useful people.

# Geography

# The Good Samaritan

## Luke 10:25–37

A teacher of the Law came up and tried to trap Jesus. 'Teacher,' he asked, what must I do to receive eternal life?'

Jesus answered him, 'What do the Scriptures say? How do you interpret them?'

The man answered, '"Love the Lord your God with all your heart, with all your soul, with all your strength, and with all your mind'; and 'Love your neighbour as you love yourself"'.

'You are right,' Jesus replied; 'do this and you will live.'

But the teacher of the Law wanted to justify himself, so he asked Jesus, 'Who is my neighbour?'

Jesus answered, 'There was once a man who was going down from Jerusalem to Jericho when robbers attacked him, stripped him, and beat him up, leaving him half dead. It so happened that a priest was going down that road; but when he saw the man, he walked on by, on the other side. In the same way a Levite also came along, went over and looked at the man, and then walked on by, on the other side. But a Samaritan who was travelling that way came upon the man, and when he saw him, his heart was filled with pity. He went over to him, poured oil and wine on his wounds and bandaged them; then he put the man on his own animal and took him to an inn, where he took care of him. The next day he took out two silver coins and gave them to the innkeeper. "Take care of him," he told the innkeeper, "and when I come back this way, I will pay you whatever else you spend on him."'

And Jesus concluded, 'In your opinion, which one of these three acted like a neighbour towards the man attacked by the robbers?'

The teacher of the Law answered, 'The one who was kind to him.'

Jesus replied, 'You go, then, and do the same.'

---

## NATIONAL CURRICULUM POINTER: GEOGRAPHICAL SKILLS (MAKING MAPS AND PLANS)

### AIM: To show that Christians should be kind to others

### INTRODUCTION

Present the children with a series of situations, and after each one ask the children who they think was being kind. You could use the situations below or make up some of your own that are appropriate for your situation.

) Three children were playing in the playground, when one fell over. One helped him get up and took him to the teacher but the other ran away.

) A girl had a bag of sweets. She dropped them all over the floor. One girl helped her pick them up but the other picked some up and started to eat them.

) Two children were fighting. One boy ran to find a teacher while another boy cheered them on.

d) A girl's pencil broke. One boy lent her a pencil but the rest laughed.

Tell the children that they are going to hear a story from the Bible. Can they work out which one of the people in the story was the one who was kind?

### STORY

**RESOURCES:** a roll of lining paper about ten feet long, four paper bags with a face drawn on each; four rulers

*Before you tell the story, you will need to draw a very simple background on the roll of lining paper. One end of the paper (about two feet of its entire length) should show a group of robbers running away. These could be very simple stick-people. The other end, again about two feet in length, should show a simple building which could be an inn. The remaining middle section should be background only, with a road running along the bottom and hills in the distance. Make four very simple puppets by*

*putting the rulers in the paper bags. If you have time, you might like to make the faces more complex by adding features such as hair and beards made from wool.*

*When you are ready to tell the story, ask for two volunteers to hold the background for you. Get them to hold the background between them but make sure that the robbers are showing while the inn scene is still rolled up. Next, ask for a further four volunteers to be your puppeteers. Give each one a paper bag on a ruler. Tell the story below. You will need to tell the volunteers what to do as the story progresses.*

One day, a man travelling from Jerusalem to Jericho was mugged. The muggers beat him up, stole his belongings and left him badly injured in the road. (*The child holding the background at the end with the robbers on it should roll up the paper till the robbers cannot be seen. One puppeteer should walk behind the background to the mid-point, then push his puppet under the paper and hold it horizontally on the background side.*)

Some time later, a priest came along. He sa[w] the injured man and walked away quickly. (*On[e] puppeteer should walk along in front of the bac[k]ground, pausing to let his puppet look at th[e] injured one before moving quickly to the end [of] the background and sitting down.*)

Later still, another person came along, looke[d] at the injured man, then walked quickly awa[y] (*Another puppeteer should walk along in front [of] the background, pausing to let his puppet look [at] the injured one before moving quickly to the en[d] of the background and sitting down.*)

The next person to travel along the road was [a] Samaritan. As soon as he saw the injured man, h[e] went up to him, did his best to clean up his injuri[es] and then took the man to a nearby inn. (*Th[e] remaining puppeteer should walk along in front [of] the background and make his puppet pause by th[e] injured man. The two puppeteers should the[n] walk their puppets along to the inn, which th[e] child at that end of the background should hav[e] unrolled while the two puppets were pausin[g] together.*)

At the inn, the Samaritan took care of th[e] injured man and the next day left money so that th[e] innkeeper could continue to take care of him. Th[e] Samaritan even promised to return and pay an[y] extra money that the innkeeper had spent on carin[g] for the injured man. (*The Samaritan puppete[er] should sit down.*)

**Now ask the children who they think was kin[d] to the injured man.** (The injured man puppete[er] should sit down.) **Tell the children how Jesu[s] told Christians that they should be kind to on[e] another. Christians today try very hard to b[e] kind to other people.**

## PRAYERS

Tell the children to be very quiet and still as you focus your collective thoughts towards God. Use one or both of the following prayers.

**Dear God,**
**There are lots of things we could do to help but we just walk by.**
**They are not difficult things and often are only very small things.**
**But if we did them, somebody's life would be made much easier.**
**They are things like putting dirty washing in the basket, not leaving it on the floor for someone else.**
**They are things like doing what we are told without arguing.**
**They are things like waiting our turn instead of pushing in front of someone else.**
**As we go through today, Lord, please help us to see the things we would normally walk past.**
**Help us to do the things we would normally not notice. Amen**

Dear God,
There are so many people who look after us and are kind to us—people like our families, our teachers, our friends.

Please help us to notice what they do and thank them, if not through our words then through our actions.

Please help us to find ways in which we can be kind to them too.

Amen

Follow up this assembly, enabling the children to practise geographical skills by using the most appropriate activities for your group from the selection below.

## ACTIVITIES

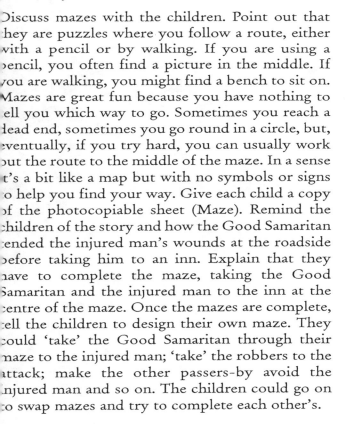

## The Good Samaritan Maze

RESOURCES: photocopiable sheet (The Good Samaritan Maze); pencils; crayons

Discuss mazes with the children. Point out that they are puzzles where you follow a route, either with a pencil or by walking. If you are using a pencil, you often find a picture in the middle. If you are walking, you might find a bench to sit on. Mazes are great fun because you have nothing to tell you which way to go. Sometimes you reach a dead end, sometimes you go round in a circle, but, eventually, if you try hard, you can usually work out the route to the middle of the maze. In a sense it's a bit like a map but with no symbols or signs to help you find your way. Give each child a copy of the photocopiable sheet (Maze). Remind the children of the story and how the Good Samaritan tended the injured man's wounds at the roadside before taking him to an inn. Explain that they have to complete the maze, taking the Good Samaritan and the injured man to the inn at the centre of the maze. Once the mazes are complete, tell the children to design their own maze. They could 'take' the Good Samaritan through their maze to the injured man; 'take' the robbers to the attack; make the other passers-by avoid the injured man and so on. The children could go on to swap mazes and try to complete each other's.

## Eagle's Eye View

RESOURCES: photocopiable sheet (Eagle's Eye View); pencils; crayons

Remind the children about the story of the Good Samaritan and how he was kind to the injured man just as God wants us to be kind and caring towards one another. Tell the children about eagles and how they would have been found in the mountainous districts of Israel. Point out that the road to Jericho from Jerusalem was very rocky and steep so there were probably eagles in the sky above the road. Give each child a copy of the photocopiable sheet (Eagle's Eye View) and ask them to colour in the picture of the Good Samaritan and the injured man. While they do so, they should look very carefully at the picture and think about what an eagle high up in the sky would have seen. Tell the children to draw on the bottom half of their sheet what they think the eagle would have seen. Point out that a plan is really just a picture of what you see from the air. Discuss the picture with the children before they begin to draw, pointing out the way the views would differ. When all the pict-ures are complete, look at them with the children and discuss plans and maps.

## Signs and Symbols

RESOURCES: paper; pencils

Review the story of the Good Samaritan with the children. Try to make it very visual by suggesting that the road from Jerusalem to Jericho was rocky and steep. It was probably quite narrow in places. There were many dangers, such as falling rocks, and muggers. But there was an inn where travellers could rest overnight. Discuss how nowadays we have road signs and symbols on maps to warn us of dangers such as falling rocks or to inform us of the whereabouts of things such as inns or hospitals. Tell the children to design the sort of road signs that would have made the traveller's journey easier in the story of the Good Samaritan. When the signs are complete, remind the children that the outward sign of a Christian should be his or her kind actions towards other people.

## Instructions Game

RESOURCES: squared paper; pencils; crayons

Before this activity, take a piece of the squared paper. Draw the traveller in the bottom left-hand corner square and the inn in the top right-hand corner square. Work out a roughly diagonal route between the two. Then work out the instructions you need to give the children, such as 'two squares up', 'three squares right' and so on. The size of the squares on the paper will determine how complex you can make the route. When you are ready to start the activity, give each child a piece of squared paper. Tell them that they are going to make a picture of the story about the Good Samaritan. Tell them that you want them to do exactly what you tell them to, so that, at the end, all their routes should look very much the same. Carefully give the children the instructions for the route you have worked out. You could ask them to colour in the squares they count, if you like, rather than simply drawing a line. Remind the children that the route from Jerusalem to Jericho was a particularly dangerous one and that the Good Samaritan was very brave to stop and help the injured man. Sometimes we have to be brave when we help another person.

## Extension Activity

If the children have been particularly interested in maps, you might like to extend their knowledge by arranging to take them orienteering. You will need to find a well-organized course that caters specifically for the right age group. Try a local park or recreation centre.

# Paul's Shipwreck

## Acts 27:1-16

When it was decided that we should sail to Italy, they handed Paul and some other prisoners over to Julius, an officer in the Roman regiment called 'The Emperor's Regiment'. We went aboard a ship from Adramyttium, which was ready to leave for the seaports of the province of Asia, and we sailed away. Aristarchus, a Macedonian from Thessalonica, was with us. The next day we arrived at Sidon. Julius was kind to Paul and allowed him to go and see his friends, to be given what he needed. We went on from there, and because the winds were blowing against us, we sailed on the sheltered side of the island of Cyprus. We crossed over the sea off Cilicia and Pamphylia and came to Myra in Lycia. There the officer found a ship from Alexandria that was going to sail for Italy, so he put us aboard.

We sailed slowly for several days and with great difficulty finally arrived off the town of Cnidus. The wind would not let us go any further in that direction, so we sailed down the sheltered side of the island of Crete, passing by Cape Salmone. We kept close to the coast and with great difficulty came to a place called Safe Harbours, not far from the town of Lasea.

We spent a long time there, until it became dangerous to continue the voyage, for by now the Day of Atonement was already past. So Paul gave them this advice: 'Men, I see that our voyage from here on will be dangerous; there will be great damage to the cargo and to the ship, and loss of life as well.' But the army officer was convinced by what the captain and the owner of the ship said, and not by what Paul said. The harbour was not a good one to spend the winter in; so most people were in favour of putting out to sea and trying to reach Phoenix, if possible, in order to spend the winter there. Phoenix is a harbour in Crete that faces south-west and north-west.

A soft wind from the south began to blow, and the men thought that they could carry out their plan, so they pulled up the anchor and sailed as close as possible along the coast of Crete. But soon a very strong wind—the one called 'North-easter'—blew down from the island. It hit the ship, and since it was impossible to keep the ship headed into the wind, we gave up trying and let it be carried along by the wind. We got some shelter when we passed to the south of the little island of Cauda.

## Acts 27:18—28:1

The violent storm continued, so on the next day they began to throw some of the ship's cargo overboard, and on the following day they threw part of the ship's equipment overboard. For many days we could not see the sun or the stars, and the wind kept on blowing very hard. We finally gave up all hope of being saved.

After those on board had gone a long time without food, Paul stood before them and said, 'Men, you should have listened to me and not have sailed from Crete; then we would have avoided all this damage and loss. But now I beg you, take heart! Not one of you will lose your life; only the ship will be lost. For last night an angel of the God to whom I belong and whom I worship came to me and said, "Don't be afraid, Paul! You must stand before the Emperor. And God in his goodness to you has spared the lives of all those who are sailing with you." So take heart, men! For I trust in God that it will be just as I was told. But we will be driven ashore on some island.'

It was the fourteenth night, and we were being driven about in the Mediterranean by the storm. About midnight the sailors suspected that we were getting close to land. So they dropped a line with a weight tied to it and found that the water was forty metres deep; a little later they did the same and found that it was thirty metres deep. They were afraid that the ship would go on the rocks, so they lowered four anchors from the back of the ship and prayed for daylight. Then the sailors tried to escape from the ship; they lowered the boat into the water and pretended that they were going to put out some anchors from the front of the ship. But Paul said to the army officer and soldiers, 'If the sailors don't stay on board, you have no hope of being saved.' So the soldiers cut the ropes that held the boat and let it go.

Just before dawn, Paul begged them all to eat some food: 'You have been waiting for fourteen days now, and all this time you have not eaten anything. I beg you, then, eat some food; you need it in order to survive. Not even a hair of your heads will be lost.' After saying this, Paul took some bread, gave thanks to God before them all, broke it, and began to eat. They took heart, and every one of them also ate some food. There was a total of 276 of us on board. After everyone had eaten enough, they lightened the ship by throwing all the wheat into the sea.

When day came, the sailors did not recognize the coast, but they noticed a bay with a beach and decided that, if possible, they would run the ship aground there. So they cut off the anchors and let them sink in the sea, and at the same time they untied the ropes that held the steering oars. Then they raised the sail at the front of the ship so that the wind would blow the ship forward, and we headed for shore. But the ship hit a sandbank and went aground; the front part of the ship got stuck and could not move, while the back part was being broken to pieces by the violence of the waves.

The soldiers made a plan to kill all the prisoners, in order to keep them from swimming ashore and escaping. But the army officer wanted to save Paul, so he stopped them from doing this. Instead, he ordered those who could swim to jump overboard first and swim ashore; the rest were to follow, holding on to the planks or to some broken pieces of the ship. And this was how we all got safely ashore.

When we were safely ashore, we learnt that the island was called Malta.

## NATIONAL CURRICULUM POINTER: GEOGRAPHICAL SKILLS

## AIM: To show Paul's trust in God

### INTRODUCTION

**RESOURCES:** travel poster or brochures of Malta

Ask if any of the children have heard of Malta. Have any of them or their relations ever been to Malta for a holiday? Tell the children that Malta is a very small island in the middle of the Mediterranean Sea. Talk about places which are in or near the Mediterranean, such as Italy or Spain or the Balearic Islands, where many of them may have been on holiday. Tell the children that in the Bible there is a story about how Paul was shipwrecked on the island of Malta.

### STORY

**RESOURCES:** photocopiable sheet (Mediterranean Map) used as an OHP slide; small boat cut out from sheet and photocopied on to OHP slide

**Tell the following story, moving the small boat cut-out along the OHP slide as you do so.**

Paul, who had taken the story of Jesus to many other countries, had been arrested by the Romans in Jerusalem. They took him to Caesarea to be judged by the governor. The governor couldn't make a decision and kept Paul in prison for two years. Eventually Paul asked for Caesar, the emperor, to judge him. The governor had to agree because Paul was a Roman citizen. Paul was taken by Julius, a Roman officer, on to a ship to start the long journey to Rome. *(Place boat cut-out on coast by Caesarea.)* First of all, the ship sailed up the coast and landed at Sidon. *(Move boat cut-out up the coast to Sidon.)* Julius was very kind and let Paul go and visit his friends in Sidon. The ship then sailed along the coast of Cyprus *(move boat cut-out along the coast of Cyprus)* and landed at Myra *(land boat cut-out at Myra)*, which was a town in Lycia. Lycia is modern-day Turkey. In Myra, the prisoners were put on board another ship which was sailing straight to Italy.

The journey became very difficult because the wind was blowing in the wrong direction. *(Remind the children that Paul was aboard a sailing vessel which had none of the equipment and technology that modern ships have.)* At last the ship managed to land on the island of Crete *(land boat cut-out on the island of Crete)* in a port called 'Safe Harbours'. They spent a long time in Safe Harbours, hoping for better weather. The ship's crew decided that they would have to spend the winter on Crete because it was too dangerous to risk sailing into the open sea. The people in charge of the ship decided that they would sail along the coast and spend the rest of the winter in a harbour called Phoenix. Paul warned them that the voyage would be very dangerous, but they took no notice.

As they sailed along the coast of Crete, past a little island called Cauda *(move boat cut-out along coast of Crete, past island of Cauda)*, a terrible gale blew up. It was so bad that the ship was thrown about on the waves and became difficult to steer. The sailors had to let the ship be blown wherever the wind took them. *(Move boat cut-out into open sea.)* They were frightened because they knew they were near some treacherous sandbanks. The sailors did not want the ship to run aground. They had to make the ship lighter, so they threw the ship's cargo overboard. The next day they needed to make the ship lighter still, so they threw some of the ship's equipment overboard too.

The storm continued and everybody became very frightened. They didn't know where they were and couldn't see the sun or the stars which they used to navigate by. Paul wasn't frightened because God had sent an angel to tell him that nobody would be killed and that he would get to Rome safely one day.

After the ship had been blown across the stormy seas of the Mediterranean for nearly a fortnight (move boat cut-out towards island of Malta), the sailors began to think that they might be near some land. But it was dead of night and they could not see. So they tied a weight on to a long rope and measured the depth of the water. They found that the water was getting shallower. They were frightened that they would be shipwrecked on rocks near the coast. The sailors decided to drop some anchors and wait for daylight to see where they were.

During that night the sailors became very scared and decided to escape in a little boat and leave the prisoners and soldiers on board the endangered ship. But Paul, who knew what was happening, said to the soldiers, 'If you let the sailors go, we shall all drown.' The soldiers cut the ropes off the boat so that it floated away before the sailors could get in it.

Just before dawn, Paul said to everybody on board, 'We must all have something to eat. We haven't eaten anything for days.' Paul found some bread, thanked God for it and began to eat. The others began to trust Paul and believe what he told them, so they all had something to eat. They realized that they needed to make the ship even lighter, so they threw some more of the cargo overboard.

By now, dawn had broken. The sailors realized that they had been right and that there was land nearby. So they determined to beach the ship on the shore that they could see. They cut off the anchors, hoisted the sail and sailed towards the shore. But they hit a sandbank and part of the ship got stuck. (Move boat cut-out towards coast of Malta, and place it at an angle to show that the boat got stuck.) The sea was still very rough and the ship was being broken up. The soldiers wanted to kill all the prisoners so that they could not escape. But Julius wouldn't let them and told everyone to jump overboard and swim to shore as best they could.

They all arrived safely on shore, just as Paul had said they would. They discovered that they had landed on Malta.

**Explain to the children that Paul was able to be so confident because he trusted in God and listened to what God told him. We too should trust God and listen to what he tells us.**

## PRAYERS

### A Responsorial Prayer

Explain that you are going to lead the children in a responsorial prayer. First, teach the response, telling the children to repeat it after you several times, before trying it on their own. Explain that you will say a sentence of prayer and, when you stop, they will answer with the response.

The response is 'Help us to trust you, Lord.'

---

**When things go wrong,
'Help us to trust you, Lord.'
When other people let us down,
'Help us to trust you, Lord.'
When things seem hard and difficult,
'Help us to trust you, Lord.'
When we feel alone and lost,
'Help us to trust you, Lord.'
When we are thrown about by the troubles of life, like Paul,
'Help us to trust you, Lord.'
Amen**

---

### A Meditative Prayer

**RESOURCES:** candle; matches; a piece of driftwood or something that has been tossed about in the sea, for instance a smooth pebble or seaweed

Tell everyone to be quiet and still as you focus your collective thoughts towards God. Light the candle and show the children the sea-related object you have brought. Explain to the children the effect the sea has had on this object through the power of the waves. Ask the children to sit quietly and look at the flame and the sea-related object and think about how the power of God can change their lives if they trust him.

After a few moments, finish the prayer time by saying aloud, 'Thank you for your power in our lives. Amen'

Follow up this assembly, enabling the children to practise geographical skills by using the most appropriate activities for your group from the selection suggested.

# ACTIVITIES

## A Map of Malta

**RESOURCES:** travel brochures; souvenirs of Malta, e.g. postcards, stamps, etc.; paper; glue; scissors; map of Malta or atlas for reference; pencils; crayons

Remind the children of the story of Paul's shipwreck near the island of Malta and how he swam ashore. Discuss modern-day Malta with the children. Have any of them been there on holiday? Do they know anyone who has been there on holiday? Explain that Malta is a popular holiday destination because of its climate and position. Tell the children that you are going to make an information map of Malta. An information map tells you about the place in a visual form. Discuss with the children the things that the map might tell you. It might show pictures of towns or ports in Malta, it might give information about seasonal temperatures, it might give you information about currency or tourism etc. Next, tell each child to draw an outline map of Malta using the resource books you have provided. The children could then begin to build up their own information map using the resources you have collected. You could extend this project by encouraging the children to collect their own information about Malta over a period of time. The completed maps would make a fascinating wall display.

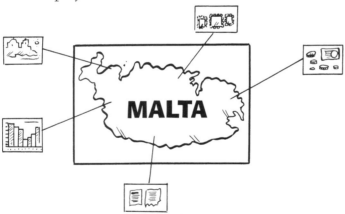

## Crete Bookmark

**RESOURCES:** photocopiable sheet (Bookmark); atlas; pencils; crayons; scissors; glue; thin card; sticky-back plastic

Discuss the route Paul's ship followed until it arrived at Safe Harbours on the island of Crete. Discuss how Paul realized that the voyage would be long and dangerous but the people in charge of the ship didn't listen and so sailed into a storm which eventually wrecked their ship. Remind the children how Paul trusted what God told him and how we too should trust God. Give each child a copy of the photocopiable sheet (Bookmark) and tell them to colour in the island of Crete, marking Safe Harbours and naming it. Remind them to colour in the sea and write the name of it. The children should then cut out their bookmark and stiffen it by sticking it on to thin card. Once the glue is dry, the children should turn the bookmark over and write on the blank side, 'Trust in God'. The children might like to decorate this phrase and cover the bookmark in sticky-back plastic to make it last longer. You might like to extend this activity by looking at the outlines of other countries such as Australia and Italy and using them to make place-mats or bookmarks with a geographical feel.

## Place Chase

Take the children to a large, open space where you can play the game safely. Tell the children that you are going to think about some of the places Paul's ship visited during the journey that ended with his shipwreck on the island of Malta. Gather the children together in the centre of the space. Explain that one side of the space will be Malta, another will be Crete, a third will be Cyprus and the final side will be Judea, where Paul's journey started. Tell the children that you will stand in the middle of the space and if you say 'Crete' they must run to that side of the space, if you say 'Judea' they must run to that side of the space, and so on. If you say the word 'Mediterranean' they must run all the way round the space and come back to you. If you wish to make this game competitive you could award a point for the first person to reach the correct space each time and a point for the first person back to you. When you have finished playing the game, remind the children of the story of Paul and how he trusted in God.

## A Route to Find

**RESOURCES:** photocopiable sheet (Mediterranean Map); pencils; crayons or felt-tips; Bible for reference

Give each child a copy of the photocopiable sheet (Mediterranean Map) and discuss how much of the story of Paul's shipwreck they can recall. Either (for younger children) read the story again, telling the children to find and circle the places on their photocopiable sheet as they are mentioned or (for older children) show them how to look up the Bible reference for themselves and do the same thing as they re-read the passage. Once the children clearly understand the route, ask them to mark the route with a brightly coloured crayon. Next, tell them to draw pictures of the ship in various places along the route; for instance, near Malta they might show the ship stuck on the sandbank, on Crete they could draw the ship docked at Safe Harbours, in the open sea they could draw the ship entering the storm, and so on. You could extend this activity by asking the children to draw a key to their map. The key should show the various positions the ship has been drawn in and give a short explanation of the meaning of each picture.

## Shipwrecked Bread

**RESOURCES:** soup; bowls; spoons; pan; bread; knives; facilities to make toast

As this activity involves food, make sure that the kitchen safety and food hygiene rules are understood and followed by everyone throughout this activity. Give each child a piece of lightly toasted bread. Show them how to cut a ship shape out of the slice. Supervise closely as they cut their own ship shapes out of their toast. Next, heat the soup and divide it between the bowls. Sit the children down and share out the bowls of soup. Remind the children of how Paul cared for his fellow sailors and encouraged them to eat by thanking God and breaking bread. Tell the children to float their ship shapes on their soup before you say Grace. Finally, share the snack of soup and 'toasted' ships together.

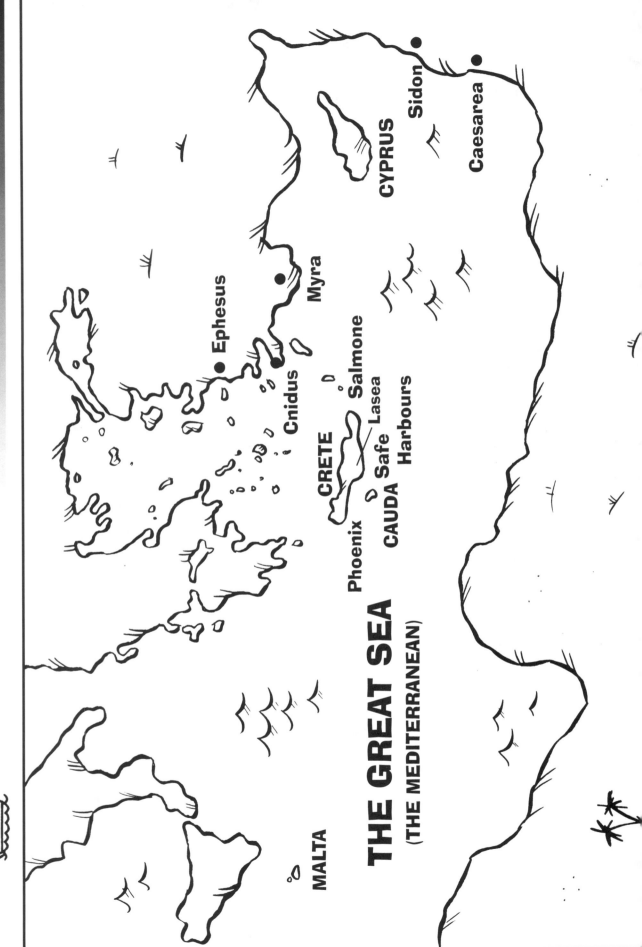

# The Wise Men and the Flight to Egypt

## Matthew 2:1–15

Jesus was born in the town of Bethlehem in Judea, during the time when Herod was king. Soon afterwards, some men who studied the stars came from the east to Jerusalem and asked, 'Where is the baby born to be the king of the Jews? We saw his star when it came up in the east, and we have come to worship him.'

When King Herod heard about this, he was very upset, and so was everyone else in Jerusalem. He called together all the chief priests and the teachers of the Law and asked them, 'Where will the Messiah be born?'

'In the town of Bethlehem in Judea,' they answered. 'For this is what the prophet wrote:
"Bethlehem in the land of Judah,
   you are by no means the least of the leading
     cities of Judah;
for from you will come a leader
   who will guide my people Israel."'

So Herod called the visitors from the east to a secret meeting and found out from them the exact time the star had appeared. Then he sent them to Bethlehem with these instructions: 'Go and make a careful search for the child, and when you find him, let me know, so that I too may go and worship him.'

And so they left, and on their way they saw the same star they had seen in the east. When they saw it, how happy they were, what joy was theirs! It went ahead of them until it stopped over the place where the child was. They went into the house, and when they saw the child with his mother Mary, they knelt down and worshipped him. They brought out their gifts of gold, frankincense, and myrrh, and presented them to him.

Then they returned to their country by another road, since God had warned them in a dream not to go back to Herod.

After they had left, an angel of the Lord appeared in a dream to Joseph and said, 'Herod will be looking for the child in order to kill him. So get up, take the child and his mother and escape to Egypt, and stay there until I tell you to leave.'

Joseph got up, took the child and his mother and left during the night for Egypt, where he stayed until Herod died. This was done to make what the Lord had said through the prophet come true, 'I called my Son out of Egypt.'

## NATIONAL CURRICULUM POINTER: GEOGRAPHICAL SKILLS

## AIM: To explore the story of Epiphany

### INTRODUCTION

**RESOURCES:** a cardboard star; a box wrapped in shiny gold paper; a ornate flask or bottle; a decorative wooden box; an large card speech bubble showing a signpost with the word 'Egypt' on it; three card crowns (keep crowns hidden from view)

Ask for eight volunteers. Give five of them one of the objects each, to hold and display to the other children. Give the crowns to the remaining three volunteers, asking them to keep the crowns out of sight. Ask if anybody can think what you might be going to tell a story about. If a child gives you the correct answer, say, 'Yes, that's right, and here are the crowns.' The volunteers can then display the three crowns. If nobody can guess the answer, say 'I'll give you another clue' and ask the volunteer to show the other children the crowns. The story should now be obvious.

### STORY

**RESOURCES:** a cardboard star; a box wrapped in shiny gold paper; an ornate flask or bottle; a decorative wooden box; three card crowns; a large card speech bubble showing a signpost with the word 'Egypt' on it; a large card speech bubble showing the words 'King Herod' crossed out

When Jesus was born, there were three wise men **(hold up the three crowns)** who spent their time studying the stars. They saw a wonderful star **(hold up star)** and realized it meant that a very special baby had been born. They decided that they must go and find this new baby and take him gifts **(hold up the three gifts)**. They lived in the east and so had a very long journey. At last they arrived in Jerusalem and went to ask King Herod where the very special baby had been born. The wise men **(hold up the three crowns)** told King Herod that they thought the baby must be the new king of Israel. King Herod was very angry and upset. He asked all his advisers where the baby was. The advisers told King Herod that this special baby would have been born in Bethlehem. King Herod went back to the wise men **(hold up the three crowns)** and told them to go to Bethlehem and find the baby. He pretended to be very interested in the baby and asked the wise men **(hold up the three crowns)** to come back after they had delivered their gifts **(hold up the three gifts)** and tell him where they had found the baby, so that he could go and visit too.

The wise men **(hold up the three crowns)** left Jerusalem to go to Bethlehem and, to their delight, they saw the wonderful star **(hold up the star)** that they had seen before, travelling in front of them. They followed the star **(hold up the star)** until it stopped moving. The wise men **(hold up the three crowns)** went inside the house that the star **(hold up the star)** had stopped over. Once inside, they worshipped baby Jesus and gave him their gifts: gold **(hold up the gold)**, frankincense **(hold up the frankincense)** and myrrh **(hold up the myrrh)**. The wise men **(hold up the three crowns)** had a dream **(hold up the speech bubble with the crossed-out words 'King Herod')** in which God told them not to go back to King Herod to tell him where the baby was. So they went home another way.

The wise men **(hold up the three crowns)** were not the only ones to be warned about King Herod in a dream. Joseph saw an angel who told him to take his wife Mary and the baby Jesus to Egypt **(hold up the speech bubble which has the signpost 'Egypt' on it)** because King Herod wanted to kill Jesus. Joseph woke up from the dream and that same night took his family to live in Egypt **(hold up the speech bubble which has the signpost 'Egypt' on it)**.

**Explain that Christians still remember these events when they celebrate the birth of Jesus at Christmas time.**

## PRAYERS

**Dear God,**
**The wise men were guided to you by a star.**
**Help us to find ways to be guided to you.**
**Help us to remember to talk to you.**
**Help us to read the Bible and find in it our way to you.**
**Help us to remember to do the things you ask us to do.**
**Help us to worship you not only on a Sunday but throughout our week.**
**Remind us to talk to people who can tell us about you.**
**Help us to be guided to you as the wise men were. Amen**

### A Rhyming Prayer

**God who made the heavens, shining up above.**
**God who sent his son to earth to bring his holy love.**
**Hold us close and near you. Help us hear you say,**
**Every child is precious in a special way. Amen**

Follow up this assembly, enabling the children to practise geographical skills by using the most appropriate activities for your group from the selection suggested.

## ACTIVITIES

### Wise Men Relay

**RESOURCES:** three crown pictures or cardboard cut-outs; three gifts; one star; one stable; a telescope. (You will need one set of these nine objects for each team)

Take the children to a large open space, where you can play the game safely. Divide the children into teams of three and remind them of the story of the wise men and their search for Jesus. Discuss each of the items with the children, explaining why they have been chosen for this game—for example, the star that the wise men followed to find Jesus. Each of the teams should line up in single file at one side of the space, opposite a chair which has been placed at the other side of the space. On the chair, place each team's set of cut-outs or pictures. Tell the children that when you say 'go', each team member in turn must run to their team's chair and collect a crown. When each member of the team has collected a crown, the first team member runs again to collect a gift. When each team member has collected a gift, the first team member runs again and this time collects one of the three remaining items (star, stable, telescope). The second team member then runs and collects one of the two remaining items. The game ends when the third team member has collected the last remaining item from the chair. Stress that no more than one person from each team can be moving at the same time. The first team to collect all their items is the winner.

### Plan to Model

**RESOURCES:** a selection of junk materials; glue; scissors; pencils; paper; card; paint; material offcuts; Christmas cards showing the Adoration of the Magi

Discuss the Epiphany story with the children and how the wise men travelled to visit Jesus. Talk about how they followed the star and went into the house to see Jesus. Explain that Epiphany comes after Christmas and, probably, by the time the wise men arrived, Mary, Joseph and the baby would have moved from the stable to a house in the town. Look at the various images on the Christmas cards that you have collected. Discuss the sort of clothes the wise men might have wor and the kind of house where they found Jesus an his mother. Tell the children either to use one c the cards as a basis for a plan of the scene wher the wise men kneel in worship or to make up thei own plan of the scene. Help the children to drav a plan, by suggesting that they think of how th scene would look if they were the star high in th sky. When the plan is complete, tell the childre to use the junk materials to turn their plan int their own very special model of the Adoration c the Magi.

### Compass Maze

**RESOURCES:** photocopiable sheet (Compass Maze); pencils; crayons

Discuss compass points with the children an how important they are when using a map. Giv each child a copy of the photocopiable shee (Compass Maze). Point out to the children th compass on the sheet. Talk about the eight point of the compass. Tell the children that they mu 'take' each wise man through the maze to his ow gift. After they have done this, they should writ out a set of instructions for each wise man's rout to his gift. The instructions should detail whic way to turn at each crossroad or junction: fo instance, 'move north from the start'; 'at the firs crossroad turn west'; 'at the second junction tur south-east'; 'when you reach the third crossroa turn north' and so on. When all the instruction are complete, the children might like to try ther out on each other to see if they are correct.

### Route to a Nativity

**RESOURCES:** paper; pencils; crayons; clip-boards

Arrange to take the children on a walk to visit nativity scene in a nearby church or shoppin centre. Make sure that you have enough adu help to carry out this activity safely. As you wall provide opportunities for the group to stop an make sketches, drawings or plans of the route an the landmarks. When you arrive at the nativit scene, discuss what you can see, pointing ou the significant characters and their part in th Christmas story. On your return to base, te the children to use the information they hav gathered to make a map of the route you followe to visit the nativity scene. If you are completin this activity at a time other than Christmas, pay visit to a local church to discover what happen there before returning to make your maps.

# Where's the Wise Man?

**RESOURCES:** photocopiable sheet (Where's the Wise Man?); crayons; scissors; large books / pieces of card (enough for one between two)

Discuss with the children the journey the wise men made and how they had to return home a different way to avoid King Herod, who wanted them to tell him where Jesus was. Discuss how hard the journey home might have been and tell the children that they are going to imagine that the wise men got separated. Give each child a copy of the photocopiable sheet (Where's the Wise Man?) and tell them that this is an imaginary map of the countryside across which the wise men may have travelled home. Tell the children to colour in the picture of the wise man, then cut it out carefully. Next, they should colour in the map. As they do this, discuss the map, making sure the children understand which parts of the map show rivers, hills, roads and bridges etc. Once the maps are complete, divide the children into pairs and explain that they are going to play a game together. They should sit opposite each other at a table with a screen between them. You could use a large book or a piece of card for the screen. Next they should put their maps flat on their side of the table, so that they cannot see each other's map. Then decide which child of each pair will give the instructions first, while the other follows the instructions. Explain that the 'instructor' places their wise man on a chosen spot on their map. The other child of the pair places their wise man at the start. The 'instructor' must then explain to the other child how to move their wise man from the start along the journey to exactly the same place as their own wise man. The 'instructor' might say, 'My wise man went along the road by the wood, he turned away from the river and walked up towards the hill. He turned right at the T-junction and stopped on the bridge over the river.' At the end of the instructions the children should compare the relative positions of their wise men.

## EXTENSION ACTIVITY

You could extend the above activity by telling the children to write a story about the wise men's journey home. They could look at the map on the photocopiable sheet to give them ideas such as crossing a river or climbing a steep hill. When all the stories are complete, you could turn them into either a book or a wall display.

# Jesus Calms the Storm

## Luke 8:22–25

One day Jesus got into a boat with his disciples and said to them, 'Let us go across to the other side of the lake.' So they started out. As they were sailing, Jesus fell asleep. Suddenly a strong wind blew down on the lake, and the boat began to fill with water, so that they were all in great danger. The disciples went to Jesus and woke him up, saying, 'Master, Master! We are about to die!'

Jesus got up and gave an order to the wind and the stormy water; they died down, and there was a great calm. Then he said to the disciples, 'Where is your faith?'

But they were amazed and afraid, and said to one another, 'Who is this man? He gives orders to the winds and waves, and they obey him!'

## NATIONAL CURRICULUM POINTER: GEOGRAPHICAL SKILLS

## AIM: To introduce the idea of Jesus as a miracle-worker

### INTRODUCTION

**RESOURCES:**

photocopiable sheet
(Introduction) used as an OHP slide

Discuss with the children journeys on board a boat. Who has been on a boat? How big was the boat? Was it a long journey or a short journey? Look at the OHP slide and discuss different kinds of boats. Point out the simple fishing boat and explain that this is the sort of boat Jesus and his friends might have used. Explain to the children that you are going to tell them a story about a time when Jesus and his friends went across a lake in a boat.

### STORY

*Tell the children that you are going to tell the story in the form of an action game. Give each class or year group a 'trigger' word. When the trigger word is used in the story, the children are 'triggered' into action. The action is to stand up, shout out their word and sit down again quickly. Alternatively, if playing with fewer children, divide the children into teams, give each child a trigger word and tell them to run around their team when their trigger word is mentioned. Tell the story of how Jesus calmed the storm as given below. The words 'water(s)', 'rocks', 'wave(s)', 'cloud(s)', 'storm', 'wind', 'breakers', 'sun', 'rolled', 'boat' and 'rain' (in bold) are the trigger words.*

One evening Jesus was sitting on board a **boat**. He said to his disciples, 'Let's sail this **boat** across the **water** to the other side of the lake.' The **boat** sailed smoothly over the **waves** in the **sun**shine. It was so calm that the disciples could see the **rocks** beneath the **water** on the bed of the lake. Jesus was very tired. He lay down with his head on a pillow and fell asleep. Suddenly a **storm cloud** appeared in the sky and the first spots of **rain** began to fall. A strong **wind** began to blow and the **breakers rolled** over the sides of the **boat**. The disciples thought their **boat** would fill up with **water** and sink onto the **rocks** below. The **wind** grew stronger and stronger, and the **rain** beat down hard. More **clouds** filled the sky and blotted out the **sun**. As the **storm** grew stronger, the **waves** grew higher and the **boat rolled** from side to side. The **breakers** were grey and cold. The disciples were very frightened but Jesus was still asleep. When they could stand the **storm** no longer, they woke him up, saying, 'Don't you know that we are in danger?' Jesus stood up and commanded the **wind**, 'Be quiet,' and he told the **waves**, 'Be still.' The **clouds** disappeared, the **sun** shone, the **rain** stopped and the big **breakers** turned into gentle rolling **waves**. Once again the disciples could see the **rocks** on the bed of the lake through the calm **waters**. Jesus said to his disciples, 'Why re you still afraid? Don't you know that I will look after you?'

The disciples were astonished and said, 'This is incredible! Even the weather does what he says.'

 **PRAYERS**

### An Action Prayer

This is an action prayer. You will need to teach the children the actions before you all say the prayer together.

---

**Thank you, God, for the story we heard.**
  God—point upwards with index finger
  story—use hands to mime opening a book
  heard—cup hands behind ears as if listening hard

**Thank you for your power that can control the sun, wind and rain.**
  power—make strongman gesture with arms
  sun—make circular shape with hands above head
  wind—sway from side to side with arms above head
  rain—mime raindrops falling, by waggling fingers as you move your hands down

**Thank you that you care for me.**
  care—cross hands across chest
  me—point with index finger to self

**Thank you that you are a God of power. Amen**
  God—point upwards with index finger
  power—make strongman gesture with arms
  Amen—bring both hands together in the traditional sign of prayer

---

### An Acrostic Prayer

**Miraculous happenings on Galilee's Lake,**
**It was late but the friends were still awake.**
**Rolling about on billow and wave,**
**All of them scared, it was a close shave.**
**'Come over here, Jesus!' they shouted out loud.**
**Long seconds later he appeared, 'midst the clouds.**
**'Enough of your fuss,' he said to the weather.**
**Stop all of this now, cease altogether.'**

**Thank you, God, for the wonderful stories of Jesus that we can read in the Bible. Thank you that they show us his might and power.**
**Amen**

---

Follow up this assembly, enabling the children to practise geographical skills by using the most appropriate activities for your group from the selection suggested.

## ACTIVITIES

## Grid Puzzle

**RESOURCES:** photocopiable sheet (Grid Puzzle); pencil; paper; crayons

This activity gives the children the opportunity to practise their skill in finding and expressing the position of a place or landmark on a map. Give each child a copy of the photocopiable sheet (Grid Puzzle). Remind the children of the story they heard, in which Jesus worked a miracle by calming the storm. Talk about the power of God and discuss other instances that we can read about in the Bible which show us his power. Explain that the sheet shows a map of the Lake of Galilee with a simple grid on it. Some of the rows have been numbered; some of the columns have been given a letter. Can the children complete the sequence? If the children know how to write down the position of a place on a map, tell them to write down the position of the place where the disciples launched their boat and the place where they landed. Ask them to guess where the storm occurred and write down its position too. If they do not yet know how to write down the position of a place on a map, show them, using the grid on the map of Lake Galilee. Afterwards you might like to go on to look at other miracles that happened on or near Lake Galilee and repeat the activity (for instance, Mark 6:45–51, which tells how Jesus walked on the water). You could complete the project by colouring in the maps and making a wall display.

## Compass Questions

**RESOURCES:** a large number of small cards, some with 'north', some with 'south', some with 'east' and some with 'west' written on them

Before you play the game, you will need to make the cards and think up a number of questions to which the answer is either north, south, east or west. For instance:

*Where did the wise men travel from?*
*East*

*Which pole do penguins live at?*
*South*

*Where does the sun rise?*
*East*

*Which compass point is directly opposite south?*
*North*

*Where does the sun set?*
*West*

*In the rhyme, what wind blows for snow?*
*North*

*Where do cowboys live?*
*(The Wild) West*

Obviously the questions should be adapted your particular group's needs and situati When you are ready to play the game, take children to an open area where there is plenty room to play the game safely. Tell the childrer form a large circle around the edge of the play area, then sit down. Number the children sequence around the circle: 1–2–3; 1–2–3, and on. Place the cards in the centre of the circle, f up so that the children can read what they s Tell the children that you will ask a question a give a number: for instance, 'What compass po is directly opposite east? Number twos.' All children who are number twos must then get and try to find a card which correctly answers question. The children should bring the card you. The first to reach you with the correct ca keeps the card. The others must return their car to the centre of the circle. The winner is the ch with the most cards at the end of the game.

## Disciple Trail

**RESOURCES:** each team will need a set of disciple cards, a card with Jesus on it photocopied from the photocopiable sheet (Disciple Trail) plus a set of cards with directional arrows on them. Each team should be given a colour and all their cards should be th colour; scissors; glue; paper; crayons/felt-tips

Before starting this activity you will need to l one trail for each team, using the arrow carc The trail should enable the team to find t twelve disciple cards and a card with Jesus on in various different places along its length. I sure you have enough adult supervision for th activity and that the playing area is safe.

To play the game, divide the children in teams. Give each team a colour and explain th they should be careful to follow only their colo trail. Along their trail they should find and colle twelve disciple cards and a card with Jesus on

When the trails are complete, each team can take their disciple cards, cut them out and make a large picture of the story in which Jesus calmed the storm. Remind the children of how frightened the disciples were when the storm suddenly blew up. Discuss with them how Jesus was able to make the winds and waves obey him.

## Signs

**RESOURCES:** card or paper; pencils; crayons/felt-tips; scissors; pictures of signs

Discuss with the children the sorts of signs that they see every day. Talk about why signs are sometimes used instead of words. Show the children some examples of signs: for instance, road signs that tell you what to do (circular) and road signs that warn you of danger (triangular). Tell the children to design some signs for your surroundings. They might give information, such as where the pencils are kept. They might warn you of danger, such as where there is a steep step. They might give you instructions, such as 'Keep to the left-hand side of the stairs'. When they are complete, you could put the best signs up in the appropriate places. Afterwards discuss with the children other signs that they might see that tell them things: for instance, the badge on a child's blazer might tell you what school they go to. The cross on the side of a building might tell you that it is a church. Ask the children if they know what sign might tell you that a person is a Christian.

Talk about crosses and the fish symbol. Refer back to the story and explain that a miracle is a sign of God's power.

## EXTENSION ACTIVITIES

### Signs

You might like to extend the activity above by talking about the different symbols used on a map to represent a church. You could study the other symbols that are used on maps and go on to ask the children to draw a map of an imaginary village using symbols to denote places such as the church, a footpath and the Post Office. You could complete the activity by asking the children to draw a picture of their imaginary village.

### What's the Weather?

Discuss various kinds of weather with the children. Point out that people wear different clothes in different sorts of weather. People also do different actions in different sorts of weather. For instance, if it is raining, people wear macs and often carry umbrellas. If it is cold and snowing, people wear warm clothes and children might throw snowballs. Explain to the children that you are going to play a game all about what people do in different kinds of weather. Take the children to an open space where you can play the game in safety. Ask the children to spread out and make sure they have plenty of space. Choose two children to be the 'mimers'. Tell them to come to you and quietly ask them to choose a type of weather they are going to mime. Tell the rest of the children that when they have watched the mime they must think what sort of weather is being mimed, then mime an action that a person might do in that kind of weather. For instance, if 'snow' is mimed they might pretend to make and throw a snowball. Play the game several times, changing the 'mimers' each time. Remind the children of the story in which Jesus performed a miracle and controlled the weather. We should always remember that our God is powerful.

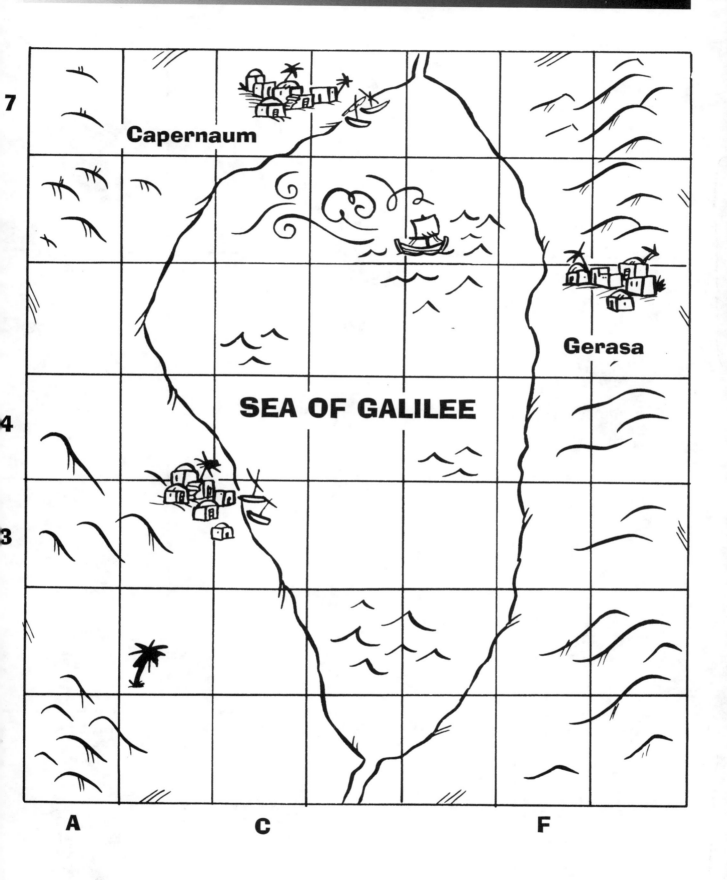

# DISCIPLE TRAIL

**Simon Peter**

**Andrew**

**James**

**Judas Iscariot**

**Philip**

# JESUS

**Simon**

**(the Canaanean)**

**Thaddaeus**

**John**

**Bartholomew**

**Thomas**

**Matthew**

**James**

**(son of Alphaeus)**

# Bible Index

This index is intended to provide a quick Bible guide, enabling you to discover whether or not a particular Bible passage is included in this book.

## Old Testament

**Bible Reference:** Genesis 6:9–22      **Noah and the Flood**
Genesis 7:11–14
Genesis 7:17–20
Genesis 8:1–19
Genesis 9:8–13

**Bible Reference:** Genesis 11:1–9      **The Tower of Babylon**

**Bible Reference:** Exodus 25:10–22      **The Covenant Box**
Exodus 20:1–17

**Bible Reference:** Deuteronomy 6:5–9      **Victorian Sunday Schools**

**Bible Reference:** 1 Samuel 17:1–17      **David and Goliath**
1 Samuel 17:20–23
1 Samuel 17:32–50

**Bible Reference:** Jonah 1:1–6      **Jonah and the Whale**
Jonah 1:11–12
Jonah 1:15
Jonah 1:17—2:1
Jonah 2:10—3:3

## New Testament

**Bible Reference:** Matthew 2:1–15      **The Wise Men and the Flight to Egypt**

**Bible Reference:** Matthew 5:14–16      **Light Under a Bowl**

**Bible Reference:** John 1:35–42      **Jesus Changes Simon's Name**
Matthew 16:13–18

**Bible Reference:** Mark 4:3–8      **The Sower**
Mark 4:13–20

**Bible Reference:** Mark 6:30–44      **Jesus Feeds a Large Crowd**

**Bible Reference:** Mark 16:15      **Saint Augustine**

**Bible Reference:** Luke 8:22–25      **Jesus Calms the Storm**

**Bible Reference:** Luke 10:25–37      **The Good Samaritan**

**Bible Reference:** Luke 19:1–10      **Zacchaeus**

**Bible Reference:** John 1:35–42      **Jesus Changes Simon's Name**
Matthew 16:13–18

**Bible Reference:** Acts 27:1–16          **Paul's Shipwreck**
                    Acts 27:18—28:1

**Bible Reference:** 1 Corinthians 11:23–25     **Jesus Shares a Meal**

**Bible Reference:** 1 Corinthians 12:12–27     **One Body with Many Parts**

**Bible Reference:** Ephesians 4:32          **The Blitz and Coventry Cathedral**

**Bible Reference:** 1 Thessalonians 5:17     **Florence Nightingale**